ONCE AGAIN IN PUBLIC EDITION

The Witches' Almanac

SPRING 2004 — SPRING 2005

For the first time combining the mysterious wiccan and arcane
secrets of an old England witch with one from New England

Prepared and edited by
ELIZABETH PEPPER and JOHN WILCOCK

CONTAINING pictorial and explicit delineations of the magical phases of
the Moon together with full and complete information about astrological
portents of the year to come and various aspects of occult knowledge
enabling all who read to improve their lives in the old manner.

The Witches' Almanac, Ltd.

Publishers   Newport

Address all inquiries and information to
THE WITCHES' ALMANAC, LTD.
P.O. Box 1292
Newport, Rhode Island 02840-9998

ISBN: 1-881098-27-3

ISSN: 1522-3183

First Printing January 2004

Printed in the United States of America

Preface

There's a natural rhythm to life on Earth. The movement of the sun and the moon set the beat, weather provides a melody, and human response lends an elusive harmony. The ancients divided the solar year into four quarters defined by the sun's journey from equinox to solstice and back again. The turning points of the cycle were celebrated, but it was the cross-quarter days that assumed the greater significance—holidays so old that their origins are lost in the mists of antiquity.

Echoing the distant past, witchcraft's Great Sabbats fall midway between seasons: the eves of February 2, May 1, August 1, November 1. Why did our forebears place such emphasis on these particular festivals? The simple truth may lie in the value of anticipation. Each celebration marks a prelude to a change of season, a time to ponder and prepare, a time to savor the expectancy. The pleasure of looking forward to an event is a reward in itself. To be alert to the shifts in time is of infinite benefit to the body, mind, and spirit.

It may be wise to heed the archaic message. Beckon February's sun with a rite of fire, collect dew at the dawn of May Day, gather in August's abundant harvest, feast, and be content to go to ground in November as dark winter sets in. You need only mind the music.

HOLIDAYS

Spring 2003 to Spring 2004

CONTENTS

ELIZABETH PEPPER & JOHN WILCOCK
Executive Editors

KERRY CUDMORE
Managing Editor

BARBARA STACY
JEAN MARIE WALSH
Associate Editors

Astrologer   Dikki-Jo Mullen
Climatologist   Tom C. Lang
Consulting Editor   Margaret Adams
Production   Bendigo Associates
Research   Susan Chaunt
Sales   Ellen Lynch

HYMN TO THE EARTH

O universal Mother, who dost keep
From everlasting thy foundations deep,
Eldest of things, great Earth, I sing of thee.
All shapes that have their dwelling in the Sea,
All things that fly, or on the ground divine
Live, move, and there are nourished—these are thine,
These from thy wealth thou dost sustain—from thee
Fair babes are born, and fruits on every tree
Hang ripe and large, revered Divinity.

The life of mortal men beneath thy sway
Is held: thy power both gives and takes away.
Happy are they whom thy mild favors nourish,
All things unstinted round them grow and flourish.
For such, endures the life-sustaining field
Its load of harvest, and their cattle yield
Large increase, and their house with wealth is filled.
Such honored dwell in cities fair and free,
The homes of lovely women, prosperously;
Their sons exult in youth's new budding gladness,
And their fresh daughters free from care or sadness
With bloom-inwoven dance and happy song,
On the soft flowers the meadow-grass among,
Leap round them sporting; such delights by thee
Are given, rich Power, revered Divinity.

Mother of gods, thou wife of starry Heaven,
Farewell! be thou propitious, and be given
A happy life for this brief melody,
Nor thou nor other songs shall unremembered be.

*The collection of literary works known as the Homeric Hymns were not written by Homer.
Scholars believe them to be poetic preludes to Greek religious festivals, probably written
down in the seventh century B. C. and apparently of far earlier origin. Shelley's superb
translations of six of the 33 Hymns brought them to the attention of English readers.*

today and tomorrow

By Oliver Johnson

ENCHANTING YOUNG WITCHES. The image of witchcraft has undergone a transformation, thanks to a number of television shows. Witches have become alluring symbols of female authority, according to media studies conducted at Warwick University in England. Popular images of witchcraft portrayed by hit shows such as "Buffy the Vampire Slayer" and "Sabrina the Teenage Witch" have altered concepts of occult figures, reports educator Rachel Moseley. No longer perceived as evil, they are regarded as sorceresses with the power to enchant and seduce; confident, independent women.

"With the exception of Harry Potter, celluloid representations of witches are typically female," says Moseley, "and historically witches have been outcasts. Much of this clearly derives from a fear of female force. The teenage witch genre articulates a new image of femininity. Witchcraft has become synonymous with power and girly magic."

DIGNIFYING WOMEN. In Australia Marguerite Johnson has been presenting much the same message at Newcastle University. She concludes that Wicca and neo-pagan movements are flourishing because they satisfy women's roles in religion far more than churches. "These beliefs resonate to the questions and feelings of a lot of contemporary women. They are very much based on worshipping earth and worshipping nature; often they are linked with environmental movements. These women have revived a lot of the pagan traditions, pagan calendars and days of worship, and take their traditions from European magic."

Johnson suggested that much of women's interest was aroused because traditional churches often didn't recognize women as priests. She also pointed out that "pioneering women came out of the sixties environment of freedom and began to set up a Wiccan religion in response to women's needs." Johnson has been trained as a classicist with studies in ancient history, Latin and Greek, and she holds a Ph.D. in Latin poetry. "But from as early as I can remember," she states, "I was fascinated with witches and wizards and loved Grimms' fairy tales."

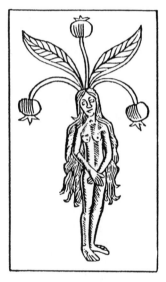

MANDRAKE ROOT FRAUD. Among other magical effects the Harry Potter phenomenon has brought to modern attention is the mandrake root. According to legend, mandrake has been considered curative since the Roman physician Pliny in the first century gave it to his patients to chew before surgery. According to Maureen Gilmer in the Ventura County Star, "In ancient times it was widely believed that a mandrake on the hearth would bring prosperity and happiness to a house, so naturally everybody wanted one." Counterfeits were appearing by the time of Henry VIII, when a fast-growing root known as bryony was doctored up at the top by inserting millet grains to form eyes, nose and mouth. The bottom half of a mandrake does indeed resemble a human body, which is probably why the ancients regarded it as cure for various sexual disorders.

TOURISTS, BEHAVE YOUR-SELVES. The spirit of a banished shaman has haunted the San Jacinto Mountains near Palm Springs for centuries, reputedly eating the souls of incautious visitors. According to the legend, Tahquitz lived three thousand years ago by the thousand-foot boulder which now bears his name. The myth has taken on new life with the opening of Tahquitz Canyon by the Cahuilla Indians. The site was closed down 35 years ago after the police moved in to evict crowds of unruly teens. But the legend persists among the Indians, many of whom give the place wide berth. Now the Cahuillas have cleaned things up and installed a visitor center where tourists can view old photographs, Indian artifacts and a15-minute film on the legend of the inhospitable Tahquitz.

THE AUSTRIAN CONNECTION.
Classes on dowsing, the Tarot and spell casting are part of the curriculum at Andreas Starchel's School of Witchcraft in Klagenfurt. No need to vanish through an underground-tube wall to locate the site, two hundred miles south of Vienna. Students learn to open their senses so they can perceive information that is filtered away by most people, says Starchel. They also learn to connect sciences in new ways. "Druids and witches are basically highly educated people, but not restricted to just one topic."

For those who live too far away to attend the monthly seminars, a correspondence course is available with seven modules, or subjects, at $230 each. At the end of each module, students whose theses pass muster receive a Certificate of Veneficia, a Latin word used to describe witches. Magic rituals work for those who believe in them, Starchel claims, because they spark two processes: selective perception and self-fulfilling prophecy. Partner Sonja Kulmitzer adds, "We want to have a quality standard. There are so many people running around claiming to be witches just because they can brew camomile tea."

SOCCER JUJU. As for players anywhere else, soccer teams in Kenya win some and lose some — but either way things get checked out with a juju man before a big match. "To depart for an international competition without consulting or including sorcerers is akin to going to an exam without a pencil," declares African Soccer magazine. Jackson Ambami is a 76-year-old "team advisor" to a variety of clubs. A typical practitioner, Ambami operates from a rundown shack in Kangemi. "Juju works," he proclaims as he drops pieces of cloth bearing the opposing team's name into a clay pot with herbs and chicken blood before heating up the stew. The Confederation of African Football takes a dim view of these practices, which it banned before a recent national championship match. "We are no more willing to see witch doctors on the pitch than cannibals at the concession stands," the organization stated.

THE MAGIC MOUNTAIN. "All my blood turned to wine and I have not been weary since," wrote naturalist John Muir when he first set eyes on Mount Shasta, California's true magic mountain. *Dweller on Two Planets* by Frederick Spencer Oliver, written in 1883, added to the site's mysterious

image. The book proposed the theory that the Lemurians, ancient survivors of Atlantis, formed a mystic brotherhood inside the 14,000-foot mountain. Muir's heady reaction to the mountain and Oliver's theory has been echoed increasingly in our own time by people with New Age perceptions. Seventeen years ago Mount Shasta caught the world's attention with the Harmonic Convergence, a gathering of psychics, mystics, healers, shamans, and UFO watchers who hoped to draw on the energies of the sacred "power spots" to bring about world peace. Many say it is time to try again.

ART FROM ATLANTIS? Smooth white stones in geometrical patterns at the bottom of the ocean off Cuba have revived speculation about Atlantis. "What we have here is a mystery," says Paul Weinzeig, spokesman for the Canadian company mapping the area on contract for Fidel Castro. "Nature couldn't have built anything so symmetrical. This isn't natural, but we don't know what it is." Anthropologist George Erikson, co-author of a book which predicted that Atlantis would one day be discovered off the coast of America, is jubilant. "I have always disagreed with all the archaeologists who dismiss myths," he states. And Erikson declares that he hopes to be the first to say, "I told you so."

BEASTLY ENTERTAINMENTS. Bears earn their nourishment by solving bamboo puzzles that dispense food. Apes admire their reflections in mirrors. Lions and tigers toy with dangling furry balls perfumed with jungle scents. Orangutans are easy to please with books and actually sit there turning the pages and looking at pictures. Many zoos around the country feature such playthings since keepers have realized that animals too get easily bored. "Behavior enrichment" is the term used by officials to describe their efforts in keeping charges happy that are deprived of the daily stimulants offered in the wild. For instance, there are better ways to feed zoo creatures than by just dumping food into cages, so often edibles are hidden. Marmosets may find theirs secreted in toilet rolls. Giraffes may discover "browse balls" of food hung in wire baskets high enough for the leggy creatures to root around in with their 18-inch tongues. "We're trying to get the animals to forage," declared keeper Megan Fox in the Los Angeles Times. "In the wild, they search all day for food. Here it's all served up."

9

Spirits of Earth   R. Anning Bell

What the heart knows today
The head understands tomorrow.
— OLD IRISH ADAGE

MOON GARDENING

BY PHASE

Sow, transplant, bud and graft			*Plow, cultivate, weed and reap*	

NEW	First Quarter	FULL	Last Quarter	NEW
Plant above-ground crops with outside seeds, flowering annuals.	Plant above-ground crops with inside seeds.	Plant root crops, bulbs, biennials, perennials.	Do not plant.	

BY PLACE IN THE ZODIAC

Fruitful Signs	Barren Signs

Cancer - Most favorable planting time for all leafy crops bearing fruit above ground. Prune to encourage growth in Cancer.

Scorpio - Second only to Cancer, a Scorpion Moon promises good germination and swift growth. In Scorpio, prune for bud development.

Pisces - Planting in the last of the Watery Triad is especially effective for root growth.

Taurus - The best time to plant root crops is when the Moon is in the sign of the Bull.

Capricorn - The Earthy Goat Moon promotes the growth of rhizomes, bulbs, roots, tubers and stalks. Prune now to strengthen branches.

Libra - Airy Libra may be the least beneficial of the Fruitful Signs, but is excellent for planting flowers and vines.

Leo - Foremost of the Barren Signs, the Lion Moon is the best time to effectively destroy weeds and pests. Cultivate and till the soil.

Gemini - Harvest in the Airy Twins; gather herbs and roots. Reap when the Moon is in a sign of Air or Fire to assure best storage.

Virgo - Plow, cultivate, and control weeds and pests when the moon is in Virgo.

Sagittarius - Plow and cultivate the soil or harvest under the Archer Moon. Prune now to discourage growth.

Aquarius - This dry sign of Air is perfect for ground cultivation, reaping crops, gathering roots and herbs. It is a good time to destroy weeds and pests.

Aries - Cultivate, weed, and prune to lessen growth. Gather herbs and roots for storage.

Consult our Moon Calendar pages for phase and place in the zodiac circle. The Moon remains in a sign for about two-and-a-half days. Match your gardening activity to the day that follows the Moon's entry into that zodiac sign.

EMPEDOCLES THE MAGICIAN

Empedocles, acknowledged as one of the most important philosophers of pre-Socratic Greece, is now more famous for his death than his doctrines. According to legend, in the ripeness of old age Empedocles flung himself into the fiery crater of Mount Etna, leaving behind only a single sandal. No comfortable, everyday sandal of leather, it was made of unyielding bronze, and like Elijah's cloak, full of meaning and power. A single brazen sandal symbolizes the goddess Hecate, she who conducts magicians along the hidden roads that join the world of the living to the worlds of the gods and of the dead. It was Hecate, we are to understand, who guided Empedocles into the otherworlds at the end of his earthly days. She did this through Fire, which is both the undermost element and the overmost. As above, so below.

Peter Kingsley published *Ancient Philosophy, Mystery, and Magic: Empedocles and the Pythagorean Tradition* in 1995. For the first time sense was made of all the strange features of Empedocles' life and writings. Kingsley showed beyond all doubt that Empedocles was not an abstract reasoner and theorist, not an armchair philosopher and poet, but a lifelong practicing magician and mystic. Nor was he the only such man among the earliest Greek philosophers. Kingsley also showed that Western rationalistic philosophy, as first articulated by Plato and Aristotle, drew its first nourishment not from the dry sands of reason and logic, but from the rich compost of experience that earlier philosopher-magus such as Empedocles had laid down through their own magic and ecstasy.

And there is more. These early Greek philosophers, as Kingsley had shown, borrowed from the magi of ancient Persia and from shamans of North Asia. The ecstatic practices of Empedocles and similar Greeks outlasted the rationalism of classical Greek philosophy. They influenced the Greek theurgists from the second century of our era to the fifth. They left substantial traces not only in the *Greek Magical Papyri*, but also in the writings of the Greek alchemists and hermeticists of Hellenistic Egypt. From these men, at Akhmim (Panopolis) in Egypt, the torch was passed to Islam by way of a few early influential Sufi teachers. And so on. The tradition of these ancient practices in all its branches spans more than 2,500 years, and its last faint echoes can still be felt today. All witches and magicians are heirs of Empedocles.

— ROBERT MATHIESEN

EMPEDOCLEAN FRAGMENTS*

Knowledge makes the mind grow.

*Let me tell you first of the sun
as the beginning of all by which
everything that we now see
became apparent.*

*At one time through Love
all things come together into one,
at another time through Strife's
hatred they are borne each of
them apart.*

*Oh, my friends, I know that
truth is with the words I shall
utter, but toilsome and heavy
and a cause of envy to men is
the onrush of knowledge into
their minds.*

*Of the roots of all things hear
me first speak: Zeus the white
splendor, Hera carrying life,
and Aidoneus, and Nestis whose
tears bedew mortality.*

*They are forever themselves, but
running through each other, they
become at times different, yet are
forever and ever the same.*

*From something not existing at
all, it is impossible that something
should grow. Total annihilation
is equally unthinkable, and 'tis
impossible it should happen, for
each thing will eternally be where
it has been set forever.*

*For I have at times already been
a boy and a girl and a bush and a
bird and a mute fish in the salty
waves.*

*The whole is a circle whose
center is everywhere and whose
circumference is nowhere.*

Die Fragmente der Vorsokratiker, H. Diels, sixth edition, revised by Walther Kranz

13

YEAR OF THE MONKEY
January 22, 2004 to February 8, 2005

They say nothing is impossible in a Monkey Year. The pace is fast, mistakes are ignored and principles set aside in favor of decisive action. An atmosphere of improvisation prevails. Fresh solutions for vexing problems are proposed. But it may be prudent to review the consequences before you gamble, for speed and enthusiasm often cloud judgement. Nonetheless, the Monkey's rule brings unexpected delights and unusual success in many ventures.

The Oriental astrological years run in cycles of twelve, each under the dominion of a symbolic creature. If you were born on or after the New Moon in Aquarius in one of the following Monkey Years, prospects are especially favorable. Enjoy a surge of energy, optimism and swift progress. Avoid overexertion.

1908   1920   1932   1944   1956   1968   1980   1992   2004

The MOON *Calendar*

is divided into zodiac signs rather than the more familiar Gregorian calendar.

2004   **2005**

 Bear in mind that new projects should be initiated when the Moon is waxing (from dark to full); when the Moon is on the wane (from full to dark), it is a time for storing energy and the wise person waits.

Please note that Moons are listed by day of entry into each sign. Quarters are marked, but as rising and setting times vary from one region to another, it is advisable to check your local newspaper, library or planetarium.

The Moon's Place is computed for Eastern Standard Time.

L E A R N I N G

Education is an ornament in prosperity and a refuge in adversity.

—ARISTOTLE

Some will never learn anything, for this reason, because they understand everything too soon.

—SIR THOMAS BLOUNT

It is impossible for anyone to begin to learn that which he thinks he already knows.

—EPICTETUS

They know enough who know how to learn.

—HENRY ADAMS

Better be ignorant of a matter than half know it.

—PUBLILIUS SYRUS

Learning is not attained by chance, it must be sought for with ardor and attended to with diligence.

—ABIGAIL ADAMS

He who would learn to fly one day must first learn to stand and walk and run and dance, one cannot fly into flying.

—NIETZSCHE

He who has imagination without learning has wings and no feet.

—JOSEPH JOUBERT

Learning without thought is labor lost, thought without learning is perilous.

—CONFUCIUS

The triumph of learning is that it leaves something done solidly forever.

—VIRGINIA WOOLF

♈ aries   March 21- April 20

Mars   *Cardinal Sign of Fire*

S	M	T	W	T	F	S
					2004 Vernal Equinox ☞	Mar. **20** ● Pisces
21 WAXING	**22** *Plan and cultivate* Aries	**23**	**24** *Look to the heavens* Taurus	**25** *Welcome beauty*	**26** *Sarah Jessica Parker born, 1965* Gemini	**27** *Smile, laugh, play*
28 ◐ Cancer	**29** *Five bright planets in a row*	**30** *Plant seeds now*	**31** *Take a chance* Leo	April **1** All Fools' Day	**2** *It is your turn* Virgo	**3** *Loosen bonds*
4 Daylight Saving 2 a.m.	**5** *seed moon* Libra	**6** WANING	**7** *Time to be brave* Scorpio	**8** *Forge ahead now*	**9** *Charles Baudelaire born, 1821* Sagittarius	**10** *Explore waste places*
11 ◑ Capricorn	**12** *Life is in an uneasy balance*	**13** *Destroy weeds and pests* Aquarius	**14**	**15** *Work a grounding spell* Pisces	**16** *Maintain poise above all*	**17** *Honor Jupiter tonight*
18 *Pay close attention to detail* Aries	**19** ●	**20** WAXING Taurus				

17

AZTEC EARTH GODDESS

The magnificent statue of Coatlicue (Co-at-lee-kway), ruler of all aspects of life, now stands in the National Museum of Anthropology in Mexico City. The abstract design and intricate carving of the stone sculpture is finally appreciated by modern sensibility and has received recognition as one of the world's great art expressions. Apart from being an artistic triumph, the work is hailed by Joseph Campbell as "an image of the universe, the goddess-mother of all being, who represents the power that generates, supports, and consumes all things on the earth-plane."

Every spring Aztecs honored Coatlicue with gifts of "flower and song," *in xochitl in cuicatl*, a metaphor for poetry, "the only truth here on earth."

taurus April 21- May 21

Venus   *Fixed Sign of Earth*

s	m	т	w	т	₣	s
			April 21 *Find a focal point*	22 *Day of glad tidings* Gemini	23 *Proceed as planned*	24 *Take a long walk*
25 *Seek Tarot insight* Cancer	26	27 Leo	28 Floralia	29 *Prepare for the feast*	30 Roodmas Eve Virgo	May 1 BELTANE ✤
2 *Catherine the Great born, 1729* Libra	3 *Hail bright Venus*	4 hare moon Scorpio	5 WANING	6 *Rain is healing* Sagittarius	7 *Unravel dream theme*	8 White Lotus Day Capricorn
9 Lemuria Honor ancestors	10 *Bono born, 1960* Aquarius	11	12 *Retrace your steps*	13 *Let fate decide* Pisces	14 *Profit by a chance encounter*	15 *Reduce speed* Aries
16 *Renew psychic energy*	17 Taurus	18 *Outwit an enemy*	19	20 WAXING Gemini	21 *Think ahead*	

Aubrey Beardsley

The Watchers

The legend of the Watchers relates how two hundred sons of heaven descended to earth and took as wives the daughters of men. The celestial beings, angels, taught their mates the forbidden arts of magic, botany, astronomy, astrology and the use of cosmetics. Azazel, leader of the Order of Watchers, instructed mankind on the manufacture and use of weapons in the art of war.

The most complete version of the tale is given in 1 Enoch, part of the Apocrypha, works not included in the Old Testament. A possible reference to the Watchers is found in Chapter 6 of Genesis: "The sons of God saw that the daughters of men were fair; and they took to wife such of them as they chose....their wives bore them children which were the mighty men of old, the men of renown." The myth is apparently a remnant of ancient Hebrew folklore. Negative elements would emerge over time. Azazel became linked to the planet Mars and warfare. The mating of angels and mortals produced giant offspring, monsters of evil. The sleepless ones, another name for the Watchers, were punished for their sins of pride and lust, sentenced to torment and eternal damnation by the all powerful Lord.

The theme of visitors from outer space is hardly unusual. Literary fantasy of science fiction has numerous examples, but folklore worldwide, oddly enough, has few. Nevertheless, the tale of the Watchers was popular during the Middle Ages. Their arrival date of June 5 was noted on calendar manuscripts of the period.

| II gemini | May 22- June 21 | | | | |  |

gemini — May 22- June 21

Mercury *Mutable Sign of Air*

s	m	T	w	T	F	s
						May **22** *Interpret your dream* Cancer
23 *Jewel born, 1974*	**24**	**25** *Observe the wild birds* Leo	**26** *Search your soul*	**27** ◑ Virgo	**28** *Learn to listen*	**29** Oak Apple Day Libra
30 *Express gratitude*	**31** *Prove your point*	June **1** *Resolve a problem* Scorpio	**2** *Thomas Hardy born, 1840*	**3** dyad moon Sagittarius	**4** WANING	**5** Watchers' Night Capricorn
6 *Be on your guard*	**7** Aquarius	**8** *Venus is a morning star*	**9** ◐ Pisces	**10** *Music lifts spirits*	**11** Aries	**12** *Avoid a pompous idiot*
13 *Profit by loss* Taurus	**14** *Practice caution*	**15** *Carry a magic charm*	**16** *Avert disaster* Gemini	**17** ●	**18** WAXING Cancer	**19** *Take a short cut*
20 Midsummer Eve	**21** SUMMER SOLSTICE ☀ Leo					

21

CELESTIAL GEMS

By consulting a wide spectrum of sources — ancient, classical, medieval, renaissance and modern — we've assembled a list of jewels most consistently linked with a particular heavenly body down through the centuries of Western occult tradition.

Agate—Mercury
Alexandrite—Mercury
Amber—Moon
Amethyst—Jupiter
Aquamarine—Venus
Beryl—Venus
Bloodstone—Mars
Carnelian—Sun
Cat's Eye—Sun
Chalcedony—Moon
Chrysoprase—Venus
Crystal—Moon
Diamond—Sun
Emerald—Venus
Garnet—Sun
Jacinth—Jupiter

Jade—Venus
Jasper—Sun
Jet—Saturn
Lapis-lazuli—Jupiter
Malachite—Venus
Moonstone—Moon
Onyx—Saturn
Opal—Mercury
Pearl—Moon
Peridot—Venus
Ruby—Mars
Sapphire—Jupiter
Sardonyx—Mercury
Topaz—Sun
Tourmaline—Mercury
Turquoise—Venus

♋ cancer · June 22- July 23

Moon · *Cardinal Sign of Water*

s	m	т	w	т	ƒ	s
		June **22** *Anne Morrow Lindbergh born, 1906*	**23** Virgo	**24** St. John's Day	**25**	**26** *Derek Jeter born, 1974* Libra
27 *Gather wild herbs*	**28** Scorpio	**29** *Train your perception*	**30** *Live in the present* Sagittarius	July **1** *Draw down the Moon*	**2** mead moon Capricorn	**3** WANING
4 *Deceit is afoot* Aquarius	**5** *Peril imminent*	**6** *Reduce risk* Pisces	**7**	**8** *Speak no evil* Aries	**9**	**10** *Express gratitude*
11 *Profit by loss* Taurus	**12**	**13** *Trust a gypsy* Gemini	**14** *Earn your wages*	**15** *Carry a talisman*	**16** *Turn over a new leaf* Cancer	**17**
18 WAXING Leo	**19** *Sweep away doubts*	**20** *Choose subject matter*	**21** *Develop a new idea* Virgo	**22**	**23** *Cast a spell* Libra	

A Loaf for Lammas

Lammas, the Great Sabbat of harvest, takes its English name from the Anglo-Saxon *hlaf-maesse*, meaning "loaf mass." The old custom of baking bread from the first ground grain and presenting it at the place of worship was an expression of spiritual thanks for a bounty. Our present-day harvests are likely to be metaphorical, but expressing gratitude for our blessings is a graceful and appropriate gesture. With that theme in mind, we offer a modern version of a harvest loaf.

1 large loaf French or Italian bread
3 ripe tomatoes, peeled and chopped
1/2 cup black olives, pitted and sliced
1/4 cup pimiento-stuffed olives, sliced
4 scallions, thinly sliced
A handful of parsley, chopped
A generous pinch of dried mint leaves,
    crumbled
A sprinkling of dried thyme
A scattering of capers
1/4 cup Parmesan cheese, freshly grated
1 tablespoon olive oil
A dash of lemon juice
Salt and freshly ground black pepper
    to taste

Cut one end from the loaf and with a long knife loosen the bread within, leaving about a half inch of crust. Scoop out the crumb into a large bowl and combine with the tomatoes, olives, scallions, parsley, mint, thyme and capers. Add the cheese, olive oil, lemon juice, salt and pepper. Mix thoroughly with a wooden spoon. Stuff the mixture firmly into the empty loaf, wrap in aluminum foil, and chill overnight.

Slice and serve as picnic fare, hors d'oeuvre or as a part of the lammastide celebration.

Note: If the tomatoes are especially juicy, you may have to add additional bread crumbs. The object is to get the stuffing moist enough but not so wet as to soften the outside crust. A delicate problem.

♌ leo — July 24 - August 23

Sun — *Fixed Sign of Fire*

S	M	T	W	T	F	S
						July **24**
25 Criss-cross, thy loss — Scorpio	**26**	**27** Gather in the harvest — Sagittarius	**28** Observe the tides	**29** Answer a clear call — Capricorn	**30** Lughnassad Eve ☞	**31** wort moon — Aquarius
Aug. **1** LAMMAS ✳ WANING — Pisces	**2** Clear the channel	**3** Martha Stewart born, 1941	**4** Billy Bob Thornton born, 1955	**5** Reverse your patterns — Aries	**6**	**7** — Taurus
8 Honor overtakes goodness	**9** — Gemini	**10** Reap herbs to store	**11** Drift with the tide	**12** Wear silver jewelry — Cancer	**13** DIANA'S DAY ✿	**14** Saturn returns — Leo
15 ●	**16** WAXING	**17** — Virgo	**18** Find the crescent Moon	**19** Pursue a fancy — Libra	**20** A red wind blows	**21** Seek an adventure — Scorpio
22 Collect fallen feathers	**23**					

25

THE VINE

Muin — September 2
to September 29

Celtic scholars now agree that the "vine" of the Druidic tree alphabet refers to the blackberry bramble bush. The sacred nature of the blackberry is evidenced in old tales and heathen customs observed down through the centuries. A loop of blackberry bramble served as a healing source in much the same way as a holed stone. Traditional rites involved passing a baby through the loop three times to secure good health. One ancient legend tells how blackberries gathered and eaten within the span of the waxing moon at harvest time assured protection from the force of evil runes. For refuge in times of danger, one need only creep under a bramble bush. In rural regions of France and the British Isles, even to the present day, it is considered dangerous to eat blackberries. The reason given in Brittany is that the fruit belongs to the fairies and they resent it when mere mortals presume to taste the magical berries.

Blackberry is one of the few plants bearing blossoms and fruit at the same time. Its curative values were many and recognized in medieval herbals. A major virtue was its reputed power to lift the spirits by restoring energy and hope. This theme persisted, for in Victorian England physicians often prescribed blackberry cordial to cheer a depressed patient.

A clue to blackberry magic may be found in a nugget of country wisdom. When frozen dew covers blackberry blossoms at dawn in early spring, farmers rejoice and hail the event as a "blackberry winter." Without this frost, the berries will not set. What may appear threatening turns out to be a blessing, for the hoarfrost is a harbinger of a rich harvest.

BLACKBERRY BRAMBLE
Rubus fruticosus

♍ virgo August 24–September 23

Mercury *Mutable Sign of Earth*

s	m	τ	w	τ	ƒ	s
		Aug. 24 *Scry for an answer* Sagittarius	25	26 *Address an issue* Capricorn	27	28 *Summon a spirit* Aquarius
29 barley moon Day of Thoth	30 WANING Pisces	31 *Time to withdraw*	Sept. 1 *Silence has no pitfalls* Aries	2	3 *A secret is a weapon* Taurus	4 *Anton Bruckner born, 1824*
5 *Raquel Welch born, 1940*	6 Gemini	7	8 *Beware of crowds* Cancer	9 *Curb a desire*	10 *From chaos comes creation*	11 Leo
12	13 *Remain aloof* Virgo	14	15 WAXING Libra	16 *Choose an element*	17 *Defend a cause*	18 *Anticipate pleasure* Scorpio
19 *Find the still point*	20 Sagittarius	21	22 Autumnal Equinox Capricorn	23 *Change is inevitable*		

To drive away demons...

Most witches have garlic in their kitchens, some have vervain, many have honey and some may even have the coveted mandrake, but every witch is sure to have salt. It is a basic ingredient in working magic. For centuries salt has been sought out and guarded by those who know its value.

A witch uses salt for many purposes, the most common being to control spirit forces. A verse referring to salt's power is found in an old English book of shadows:

Sprinkle round about ye hearth
Keep ye spirits at their bay

Evil spirits and demons are said to be about when we accidentally spill salt. For this reason, we toss a pinch over our left, or sinister, shoulder with our right hand. The baneful spirit must then count each grain before being a nuisance to us again. Some traditions even say that evil resides over our left shoulder and that the tossing of the salt will drive the spirit away.

When placed in water, salt releases its cleansing properties. In the household, a bit of salt in your cleaning solutions assures physically and spiritually cleansed living quarters.

Add salt to your bath. This is especially effective during the fourth quarter of the moon when spirit activity is at its peak and we are most sensitive.

A pinch of salt can be used to keep all manner of evil in check, whether it is a pesky ghost or a bothersome relative. Salt forms a mystic barrier between the invasive and the defending forces. It can be sprinkled on property borders to keep an annoying neighbor away. Placed between two people at a dinner table a saltcellar prevents harsh conversation or bad wishes. A touch of salt on the tongue discourages nightmares.

Salt is a symbol of purity and the embodiment of the Earth element. As such salt is ideal for grounding. It is often used to bind a spell. When the working is finished, the object can be buried in salt or placed upon a bed of salt to assure success.

There are three times when the use of salt is forbidden: before or during a séance, at the Hallows Sabbat, or in the meal of a dying person. In all three cases the presence of spirits is desired.

— THEITIC

28

s	m	τ	w	τ	f	s
					Sept. **24**	**25**
					Visit a sacred site Aquarius	*belle hooks born, 1952*
26	**27**	**28**	**29**	**30**	Oct. **1**	**2**
Speak last, spell holds fast Pisces		**blood moon** Aries	**WANING**	*Dismiss the calculator*	*Keep your distance* Taurus	*Beguile with wit*
3	**4**	**5**	**6**	**7**	**8**	**9**
Spend time alone Gemini	*Avoid a backlash*	*Shun extreme action*	Cancer	*Nature is never precise*	Leo	*Collect acorns*
10	**11**	**12**	**13**	**14**	**15**	**16**
Peter Coyote born, 1942	*Wear a talisman* Virgo		Libra	**WAXING**	*View the Milky Way* Scorpio	*Signs are favorable*
17	**18**	**19**	**20**	**21**	**22**	**23**
Sagittarius	*Try a new approach*	*Perform a fire rite* Capricorn		*Resist greed* Aquarius	*Restore psychic power*	*All things flow into form*

libra

September 24– October 23

Venus   *Cardinal Sign of Air*

29

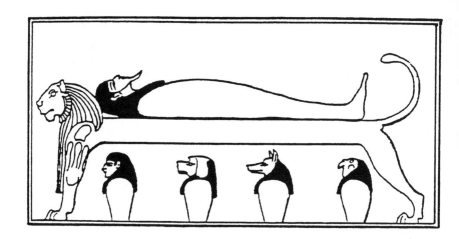

THE SONS OF HORUS

In Egyptian tombs the internal organs of the deceased were stored in four canopic jars, named after an ancient town in the Nile Delta. The receptacles, intended to preserve the viscera, were in early times plain covered vases of marble, earthenware or wood. Later, during the Middle Kingdom, the lids had human heads, often portraits of the dead. But Egypt's funerary customs became decidedly more elaborate with the advent of the New Kingdom. It was then that the covers of the canopic jars portrayed the four sons of the great solar god Horus and represented the cardinal points of the compass. The heads depicted were human, baboon, jackal, and falcon. These primary guardians were in turn watched over by four goddesses.

❋ ❋ ❋ ❋

IMSETY'S head represents the human guardian. His compass point is South, Isis is his safeguard. The greatest of all Egyptian goddesses, Isis is called the "Lady of Enchantments" and "mother to all who worship her."

HAPY has the head of a baboon, an animal highly revered by Egyptians for its intelligence. He represents the North and his protector is Nephthys. While Isis symbolizes light, her sister Nephthys denotes darkness, a darkness without evil aspects. If Isis is substance, Nephthys is shadow.

DUAMUTEF is portrayed as a jackal and belongs to the East. Guardian Neith is one of the oldest deities of Egypt, her worship extending back to predynastic times. Associated with hunting, her emblems are a bow and arrows. The art of weaving is one of Neith's domains.

QEBEHSENUEF bears the head of a falcon. His cardinal point is West and Selket, the scorpion goddess, watches over him. The benevolent Selket, despite her poisonous symbol, is noted for her magical healing powers.

scorpio — October 24-November 22

Pluto — *Fixed Sign of Water*

s	*m*	*t*	*w*	*t*	*f*	*s*
Oct. **24** *A brown wind sighs* Pisces	**25**	**26** *Dance to a moon song* Aries	**27** snow moon Total Lunar Eclipse	**28** WANING Taurus	**29** *Trust your heart*	**30** *Prepare for the Sabbat* Gemini
31 Samhain Eve *Gain one hour*	Nov. **1** HALLOW-MAS ✳	**2** Cancer	**3** *Use common sense*	**4** *Return a favor* Leo	**5**	**6** *Your character is your fate*
7 *Marie Curie born, 1867* Virgo	**8** *Find peace in music*	**9** *Let chance be your guide* Libra	**10**	**11** *Kurt Vonnegut born, 1922* Scorpio	**12**	**13** WAXING
14 *Suffer a fool gladly* Sagittarius	**15** *Find a clear horizon*	**16** HECATE NIGHT ✳ Capricorn	**17** *Plan a journey*	**18** *Extend your senses* Aquarius	**19**	**20** *Water never dies* Pisces
21	**22** *Turn the world around* Aries					

Aesop's Fables   Ulm, 1476

The Ox and the Frog

ONCE an ox came to drink at a pond. Two frogs were sitting by the pond and one said to the other: "I can be just as big as that ox!" And he huffed and puffed until he was twice his own size. But that wasn't nearly big enough. So he went on, huffing and puffing, until he exploded.

MORAL: Pretending you are something you are not can lead to disaster.

sagittarius November 23-December 21

Jupiter   *Mutable Sign of Fire*

s	*m*	*т*	*w*	*т*	*ƒ*	*s*
		Nov. **23** *Smoke betrays fire*	**24** Taurus	**25** *Mend a broken heart*	**26** oak moon	**27** WANING Gemini
28 *Mask your attitude*	**29** *Consult an elder* Cancer	**30**	Dec. **1** *Recall the past*	**2** *Beware of little sins* Leo	**3** *Reason stronger than anger*	**4** Virgo
5 *A lie is a heavy burden*	**6**	**7** *Fire enhances perception* Libra	**8** *There is world enough and time*	**9** *Find a hidden path* Scorpio	**10** *Move to higher ground*	**11** Sagittarius
12 WAXING	**13** *Steve Buscemi born, 1957* Capricorn	**14** *There is but one of you in all of time*	**15** Aquarius	**16** *Assume control*	**17** Saturnalia Pisces	**18**
19 *Edith Piaf born, 1915* Aries	**20** Yule Eve	**21** WINTER SOLSTICE				

DO NOT DISTURB

Greek myths tell of Nyx, goddess of night, who mates with Erebus, personifying the darkness of the underworld. Together they spawn a flock of shadowy, black-winged creatures: the Oreiroi, or dreams. Hypnos, god of sleep, is one of the brood along with his twin brother Thanatos, god of death. The Oreiroi enter the human mind through either a gate of ivory signifying deceit or a gate of polished horn representing truth.

Ancient Greek literature inspired the Roman poet Ovid to write *Metamorphoses*, his own version of the old tales. Ovid names the god of sleep Somnus, father to three sons who deliver dreams to mortals — Morpheus, who calls up human images to the dreamer; Phobetor, in charge of animal shapes; and Phantasus, purveyor of all inanimate things.

Classical sources consider Hypnos/Somnus a minor god of benevolent character. Hesiod described him, "Across the earth and the wide sea-ridges, Hypnos goes his way quietly back and forth, and is kind to mortals." An Orphic Hymn praises the god of sleep, "Sovereign of all, sustained by mother-earth; for thy dominion is supreme alone, over all extended, and by all things known." And in Ovid's words: "Somnus, quietest of gods, Somnus, peace of all the world, balm of the soul, who drives care away, who gives ease to weary limbs after the hard day's toil and strength renewed to meet the morrow's tasks."

At times the realm of sleep can be maddenly inaccessible. As witness the prayer of a 1st century insomniac: "O Somnus, gentlest of the gods, by what crime or error of mine have I deserved that I alone should lack thy bounty? ...Touch me but with thy wand's extremest tip — 'tis enough — or pass over me with lightly hovering step."

Old witch lore compares going to sleep with passing through a door. We often slip through, barely aware of the transition. But most of us know the fitful state that occasionally occurs when the door is locked. All efforts to find the key are in vain. Troubling thoughts replace sound judgement as anxiety takes free rein. Your mind has become a wild creature caught in a trap. Your task is to free it from torment.

Sympathic magic is a practical way to deal with sleeplessness. Waste no time tossing and turning. Gather your thoughts together and clearly identify them on a sheet of paper. Describe the fears or frustrations churning in your brain. Once committed to writing, the worry assumes a new form — a true metamorphosis. Fold up the document and place it in a lidded box or drawer. Return to bed and visualize an open door. Cross the threshold to find peace in the sweet land of Somnus.

♑ capricorn December 22- January 20

Saturn   *Cardinal Sign of Earth*

s	m	T	W	T	F	s
			Dec. **22** *Heed a warning* Taurus	**23**	**24** *Enliven spirits* Gemini	**25** *Express a wish*
26 wolf moon Cancer	**27** WANING	**28** *A white wind sings*	**29** *Expose a rascal* Leo	**30** *Answer a call for help*	**31** *Join the chorus*	Jan. **1** 2005 Virgo
2 *Open a new door*	**3** ◖ Libra	**4** *As above, so below*	**5** *Thoughts are things* Scorpio	**6**	**7** *Katie Couric born, 1957* Sagittarius	**8** *Concede minor point*
9 Day of Janus Capricorn	**10** ●	**11** WAXING Aquarius	**12** *Cherish a friend*	**13** *Learn to be vague* Pisces	**14**	**15** *A lucky day for all*
16 *Attract attention* Aries	**17** ◗	**18** Taurus	**19** *Robert E. Lee born, 1807* Gemini	**20** *Solve a puzzle*		

TOWER OF THE TAROT

The tower is a powerful and dangerous card. Whether upright or reversed in a Tarot reading, the meaning is one of unavoidable disaster. Adjacent cards may inform but fail to nullify its dire force.

Through centuries of Tarot history, the graphic depiction of the card has remained remarkably similar. Atop a strongly built tower with three portals is a crown struck by a bolt of lightning. Two figures, male and female, are thrown to the ground. A series of dots, in some designs tiny perfectly formed circles, fall from above.

The card has various names, including the House of God, the Tower of Destruction, the Hospital—in its original meaning as a place of shelter for travelers—and the Tower of Babel. The last is an allusion to the bibli-cal explanation for the diversity of tongues. A divine decree held that a single language shared by all would engender human ambition.

Hypocrisy revealed by a dramatic event is a constant theme. One interpretation calls the Tower an illusion — an imaginary monument built by human desires. Another source defines it as a fortress of thought or opinion with the crown as its pride and glory. A cataclysm demolishes an institution's prestige, causing ruin and social upheaval. The rain of dots, fallout from the disaster, represents a triumph of truth over false principles. A keen observer notes that while the crown is dismantled, the tower is left intact. Its identifying feature, the three windows stand for pride, ignorance and hubris — difficult sins to erase.

aquarius **January 21-February 19**

Uranus   *Fixed Sign of Air*

s	m	t	w	t	f	s
					Jan. **21** *Learn a new song*	**22** *Jim Jarmusch born, 1953*
23 *Jeanne Moreau born, 1928* Cancer	**24**	**25** (storm moon) Leo	**26** WANING	**27** *Once bitten, twice shy*	**28** *Take a deep breath* Virgo	**29** *View life from a hilltop*
30 Libra	**31** *Truth is elusive*	Feb. **1** Oimelc Eve Scorpio	**2** CANDLEMAS	**3** *Lighten your burden*	**4** *Visualize a new you* Sagittarius	**5** *Search the shadows*
6 *Discretion is a wise choice* Capricorn	**7**	**8** Year of the Cock Aquarius	**9** WAXING	**10** *Things go well tonight* Pisces	**11** *Flow with the tide*	**12** *Begin a quest* Aries
13 *Lead the way*	**14** *Raise the level of play* Taurus	**15**	**16** Gemini	**17** *Grasp the nettle and work*	**18** *Stillness clears muddy water*	**19** Cancer

The Hidden Language of the Quipu

Alone among Bronze Age civilizations, the Incas of Peru had no written language — but according to a recent book their system of recording events was very similar to that of present-day computers.

The Incas' instrument of record was the quipu, a bundle of knotted strings of various lengths and colors that encoded "expenditures or other things that had taken place many years before. By these knots they counted from one to ten and from ten to a hundred, and from a hundred to a thousand. On one of these strands there is an account of one thing, and on the other of another, in such a way that what to us is a strange, meaningless account is clear to them."

The words are those of Pedro de Cieza de León, a Spanish explorer whose 17-year exploration of Peru led to his 1550 book *The Incas*, published by the University of Oklahoma in a 1959 edition. That description of the quipu is the earliest on record.

About five hundred quipu have survived to present times, many preserved in the American Museum of Natural History in New York. But the quipucamayocs, who were specially trained to keep and interpret these records, are long gone. And, lacking the equivalent of a Rosetta Stone, nobody knows how to read them today, apart from their recognition as "ingenious mnemonic devices."

In 2003 the University of Texas published *Signs of the Inka Khipu* by Dr. Gary Urton, a Harvard anthropology professor. He reiterated that the Incas manipulated strings and knots to encode and store information in a shared system of record keeping and concluded that the knots appeared to be arranged in coded sequences analogous to the "process of writing binary number (1-0) coded programs for computers."

Other researchers have also recently suggested that as many as 20 percent of existing quipu were "clearly non-numerical" and could have been examples of an early form of writing. According to Pedro de Cieza de León's description of 450 years ago, "This orderly system in Peru, is the work of the Lord-Incas who ruled it and in every way brought it so high, as those of us here see from this and other great things."

Art by Peruvian native Poma de Ayala (1535-1616), lost for centuries but rediscovered in Denmark in 1908, shows an Inca using a quipu.

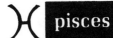 **pisces** February 20 - March 20

Neptune   *Mutable Sign of Water*

s	*m*	*τ*	*w*	*τ*	*F*	*s*
Feb.**20** *Discover a new route*	**21** Leo	**22** *Walk on the edge*	**23** (chaste moon)	**24** WANING Virgo	**25** *Enrico Caruso born, 1873*	**26** *Act quickly now* Libra
27 *Rectify a wrong*	**28** *Study old lore*	Mar.**1** Scorpio	**2** *Find a hidden symbol*	**3** ◐ Sagittarius	**4**	**5** *Measure your pain* Capricorn
6 *Forgive an error*	**7** Aquarius	**8** *Delay decision*	**9** *Counter a curse* Pisces	**10** ●	**11** WAXING Aries	**12** *Faith does wonders*
13 *Prefer solitude* Taurus	**14** *Enjoy a privilege*	**15**	**16** *Answer a distress call* Gemini	**17** ◐	**18** *Queen Latifah born, 1970* Cancer	**19** *Pay in advance*
20 *Life begins anew* Leo						

39

From Grünbeck's *New Interpretation of Strange Miracles*   Mainz, 1507

A PREVALENCE OF CROSSES

Whoever fights monsters should see to it that in the process he
does not become a monster. And when you look long into an
abyss, the abyss also looks into you.

— NIETZSCHE
Beyond Good and Evil

Window on the Weather

We are transfixed by the colorful representations of our daily weather experiences as they are represented on our televison screens. We are intrigued with lively maps, illustrations, and motions; plenty of excitement and mystery are conveyed. The future seems questionable as well as our security in relation to the elements. But reality is quite different – the weather is mostly safe, fun, interesting and sometimes adds to our family legacy of memories. Who could forget the big snowstorm that kept us together indoors for three days back in '65? Or that fine spring day in the park when I met you. The fall colors were especially marvelous that homecoming weekend when we beat – what was that town's name? Seems we can't always remember the details of the day or month or season, but we always seem to remember the weather. And we can evoke what it stirred in us no matter where we were in our lives. Think of such events as calling cards from the past to remind us of how we have been shaped. The elements experienced truly are the raw material of our spirits.

— TOM C. LANG

SPRING

MARCH 2004. After late winter thaw, snowy and cold conditions return to the East for one last volley. A wet, heavy snowfall clogs Northeast and interior mid-Atlantic travel around the 20th. Unusually cold weather slows what would normally follow as an orderly snowmelt. Energy costs remain high from the Great Lakes to the Northern Plains. Snowfall is heavy in the Rocky Mountain West with at least two Pacific born storms bringing rain and wind down the entire West Coast. These full latitude storms will also bring deep snowfalls to interior mountain ranges from Washington State to extreme southern California.

APRIL 2004. Slow moving and large circulation cyclones will bring long spells of rain and wet snow to the Northeast. Though generally limited to inland communities, a surprise spring snowstorm cannot be ruled out through the Boston to New York corridor. Any warming sunshine will be brief and followed by more chilly rains in that area. Farther west, the Great Lake States enjoy partly sunny and chilly early spring weather with only brief encounters with stray showers. The Great Plains are cool and dry. Tornado-producing thunderstorms sweep through Texas and Oklahoma. Rocky Mountains snows are plentiful this year, especially in Colorado. West Coast weather becomes quiet, though the prevailing Pacific Coast breezes are notably present.

MAY 2004. May is usually the likeliest time for tornadoes, particularly in the Midwest and Great Plains. This year's activity will be more numerous and widespread than usual. A broad airflow emanating from the Pacific Ocean will carry east and spawn these dangerous storms, especially between 4 p.m. and 8 p.m. Though most of us will never be impacted by a tornado, it is wise to remember that a tornado can strike at any time following a violent thunderstorm and is located on the southwest side of such a storm. The safest sanctuary from powerful winds is in a reinforced interior room or basement and away from windows. Temperatures will be pleasantly mild throughout much of the country. The Rockies will have another round of heavy snow and the Northeast can expect a freak late-season winter storm.

SUMMER

JUNE 2004. As the spring passes into summer, June will be remembered for its moderate turn from warmth to heat in the West. An ominous tone is set there as a few wildfires flare in the mountains of Montana and Idaho. Residents are served well to remember last year's conflagrations and stay prepared, ready to move on a moment's notice. Elsewhere conditions are more temperate. Rainfall arrives at a furious rate, occasionally and only briefly from West Virginia to Georgia and mostly in higher terrain. Florida thunderstorms form away from the coast with Orlando struck most often and mainly during the afternoons. The Northeast enjoys warm days and pleasant evenings with the last of the two-blanket nights having passed. Midwest crop yields will be abundant this summer.

JULY 2004. Temperature extremes, both hot and cold, occur one month after the summer and winter solstices. Not only do the hottest and coldest days of the year transpire at this time, but the potential to experience temperatures well above their normal highs and lows occurs as well. The greatest potential for record-setting temperatures will be in the West this year, especially in Washington and Oregon, where another warm, dry summer is likely. Many sunsets will be accompanied by splendid views of Mt. Rainier, Mt. Hood and Mt. Bachelor. Farther east, rainfall is heavy and relatively long lasting in the Southeast, and a monsoon flow will form and bring substantial wet weather to the Ohio Valley and Northeast. Several early season easterly waves bring downpours to Florida. A severe weather outbreak brings high winds and an isolated tornado to central New England.

AUGUST 2004. Because of the general warmth that exists north to south and from coast to coast, jet stream winds are light during August. As a result, weather systems move slowly at this time. Where rainfall occurs it lasts a long time, often for hours. Meanwhile just a short distance away clouds can be seen and thunder heard, but no rainfall may arrive. This is especially true in the South and notably in Florida, where thunderstorms cast an immense shadow daily over afternoon plans. Respect the hazard from lightning there, as it can strike as much as ten miles away from its emanating thunderstorm. The tropical hurricane season stirs to life with the first disturbances forming in the western Atlantic Basin. This area includes the Caribbean, Gulf of Mexico and the Bahamas. The West Coast enjoys some wonderful summer weather. Big ocean swells arrive for southern California surfers, courtesy of an offshore tropical storm.

AUTUMN

SEPTEMBER 2004. Historically hurricanes follow migration routes that follow decade-long patterns. For example, the forties and fifties produced a great number of hurricanes along the East Coast, while the sixties and seventies saw very little activity. What determines these trends is not altogether clear, yet there are some hints. The notion is new to meteorology that there are a number of monsoons, or more specifically moisture channels, that occasionally appear on the southeast part of continents in the Northern Hemisphere. Hurricanes are more likely during these times. Such was the case last year and whereas these particular monsoons tend to stay in place for several years at a time, we can surmise that once again the East Coast will be susceptible to a hurricane this September. Otherwise the month is quite pleasant across the rest of the country with an early snowfall likely in the Rockies around the 15th.

OCTOBER 2004. This will be a particularly quiet month throughout the country. As noted earlier, midsummer and midwinter usually show the greatest deviations away from normal cold and warmth. Conversely temperatures tend to be the most consistent during both spring and fall. Stray cold snaps and heat waves tend to be short lived and with very little moisture available during October, not much rain and snowfall can be expected. Still there will be suggestions of the season to come. First snows will dust both the Rockies and northern Appalachians. There tourists will delight in spectacular fall colors. The fire danger only diminishes in the West on the arrival of the season's first snowfall.

NOVEMBER 2004. Only a significant volcanic eruption will alter what will likely be another early winter. Based on recent research, forecasters realize that while volcanoes contribute to global cooling, sometime after an initial eruption the first affect is actually a brief warming in the atmosphere. This is because of the emission of sulphur dioxide, a greenhouse gas. After a season or so of warmer weather, the cooling affects of a volcanic eruption will occur. It is notable that based on climatological data, a meaningful volcanic eruption often occurs one to two years after a solar cycle of maximum heat. This event took place about 18 months ago. We may reasonably expect a mild start to this year's winter season. Snow and cold are moderate this November as a Pacific airflow crosses the country. This will generally bring balmy temperatures and above normal rainfall. Expect an early ski season in the Rockies and Sierra Nevada of California.

WINTER

receive the lion's share of snowfall with fine skiing from Utah to Montana. Coastal cities in the East will probably be snow free, except for the occasional dusting. Energy bills can be as much as 40 percent lower than last year. January is not noted for severe weather, yet Oklahoma and Texas will be visited by a brief and sporadic tornado outbreak at midmonth. The West will receive its share of rain. In fact, Southern California runs the risk of mudslides from several soakings.

DECEMBER 2004. Great Lake residents are gleeful at the prospect of a snow free early winter. This occurs with one exception. A southwest wind, generally balmy, brings a sudden deep snowcover to Buffalo, N.Y. Maybe up to two feet! Fear not, however, as warmer weather will soon follow and bare ground will return in less than a week. Snowfall is scarce elsewhere. Only the Pacific Northwest and northern Rockies experience anything close to normal early winter weather. In fact, temperatures are so mild that residents coast to coast will save on energy bills as both the price and volume of oil consumed will be much less than the past two years. West Coast storms will bring green grass and quell the fire danger. Georgia and Florida are quite dry this year.

JANUARY 2005. The January thaw will be far more extensive this year as balmy breezes blow mild air from the Pacific Ocean across the country. Arctic air is trapped in Canada with only occasional and brief excursions into the U.S. The northern Rockies will

FEBRUARY 2005. Mild and wet will be the national weather pattern this February. Snowfall will increase somewhat, but most severe cold will stay north of us. From the Appalachians to southern New England a heavy wet snowfall will occur around the 10th, without much wind and cold. Trees will lay heavy with snow for several days, but milder days will bring bare ground once again within a week. Only the mountainous West will have a lasting snowcover this winter, much of it above eight thousand feet in the Rockies. Florida will be experiencing a passing squall line, briefly producing high winds and an isolated tornado. Rainfall is generally heavy in the Southeast with double the normal rainfall. Southern California is drenched too, with occasional mudslides making headlines. Heavy surf there driven by stiff winds off the Pacific.

Toads and Diamonds

Once upon a time there was a widow who had two daughters. The elder was just like her mother in face and in manner, and both were so disagreeable and so rude that there was no living with them. The younger took after her father, who had been kind and sweet-tempered, and she was very beautiful as well.

As people naturally love those in whom they see themselves, this mother was foolishly fond of her elder daughter, and at the same time had a deep dislike of the younger. She made her eat in the kitchen and work from daylight till dark.

Among other tasks, the child was forced to go twice a day to a spring over a mile and a half from the house and bring home a heavy clay pitcher full of water. One morning as she stood resting by the fountain, an old woman hobbled up to her and begged for a drink.

"Oh, yes, with all my heart, ma'am," said the kind girl, and rinsing out her pitcher, caught the clear, cool water as it bubbled forth from the rock and gave it to her, holding up the pitcher all the while that the old woman might drink more easily.

Refreshed by the sweet water, the beggar leaned on her staff and said, "You are so good and thoughtful, my dear, that I will reward you." For this was a fairy, who had taken the form of a shabby old cripple to see whether the girl was as sweet as she looked. "I will give you for gift," continued the fairy, "at every word you speak there shall come out of your mouth either a flower or a jewel."

When the girl reached home her mother scolded her for staying so long at the fountain. "Please forgive me, mother," pleaded the child. And as she spoke there fell from her lips a rose, two pearls, and a sparkling diamond.

"What is this I see?" cried the mother, quite astonished. "Am I bewitched or did I really see pearls and a diamond fall from your mouth? What does it mean, my child?" This was the first time she had ever spoken to her younger daughter so tenderly.

The girl told her all that had happened, and at every word a ruby, an emerald, a sapphire, or a lovely flower fell from her lips.

"This is wonderful!" declared the mother. "I must send your sister to the fountain. Fanny, come here! See, my precious, what comes out of your sister's mouth when she speaks. Would you like to have the same gift given to you? You need only go to the fountain, and when a poor old woman asks you

46

for a drink, give it to her very politely."

"Do I look like a servant?" asked the rude girl. "Why should I carry a heavy pitcher to the spring for water?"

"You shall go, you bold child," snapped her mother, "and go at once." So away she went, grumbling all the way, carrying the best silver tankard in the house. As she stood by the fountain she saw coming out of the woods a splendidly dressed woman, who approached her and gently asked for a drink. This was, you must know, the very same fairy who had appeared to her sister, but had now taken on the form and dress of a lady, to see just how far this young woman's rudeness would go.

"And why should I draw water for you?" was the girl's saucy reply. "Here is the pitcher, you can stoop down and draw water for yourself, if you so choose."

"Your manners leave much to be desired," said the fairy in a quiet voice. "Well, then, since you are so insolent and unkind, I give you for gift that at every word you speak there shall come out of your mouth a snake or a toad."

As soon as her mother saw her favorite coming, she held out her hands to catch the jewels, crying: "Speak, daughter, speak."

"Speak what?" answered the girl. And with those words there dropped from her mouth a toad and a viper.

"Oh, mercy on us," gasped the mother. "It is that wretch, your sister, who has caused this." And seizing a stick, she ran to beat her. Hearing this, the poor child fled into the forest to hide.

The King's son, riding through the woods, heard sobbing and found her crying in a hawthorn thicket. "My pretty maid," he said, leaning from his saddle, "why are you here alone with night coming on?"

"Oh, sir," replied the girl, "my mother had turned me out." And as she told the whole story the Prince, who had already fallen in love with her beauty, saw all manner of flowers and jewels slip from her lips. Considering with himself that such a gift was far greater than any marriage portion he might receive from a princess, he lifted her on to his horse and took her to the royal palace. There they were married amid great rejoicing.

As for her sister, she was so hateful that her own mother finally turned her out. The miserable girl wandered about for a while without finding any one willing to take her in. At last she retreated to a corner of the wood, and there died.

This tale, drawn from an oral source, is part of the collection of French folklore published by Charles Perrault in 1697.

Illustrations by G. P. Jacomb Hood, 1889

The Mischievous Leprechaun

Leprechaun sightings have been few and far between lately, but images of the wee creatures are ubiquitous in Ireland. You can have sightings on tea towels, postcards, plates, mugs, refrigerator magnets or in films and cartoons. The size varies from small enough to be hand held to the height of a two-year old child. The "national elf" is usually shabbily dressed in an old green jacket, red breeches, woollen stockings, and shoes with big silver buckles. He wears a porkpie hat, a felt fedora flattened at the crown.

An old man in County Fermanagh has an interesting explanation of the short stature: "At one time they were as tall as you or I," he assures us. "But that was when they were at the height of their power and were greatly feared across the world. They were gods then, do you see? When the people stopped believing in them, stopped worshipping them, leprechauns began to shrink away until they reached their present size. That's why they are so small nowadays."

But some people still believe they exist. A farmer may avoid a "fairy fort" with his tractor, expecting bad luck if he destroys the site. A factory cannot be built where a certain tree stands and must not be destroyed lest he annoy fairies. Where grass refuses to grow are believed to be leprechauns' homes, and stepping on the bare patches puts an unwary pedestrian in the leprechaun's power. The only remedy for release is to turn one's coat inside out.

In the *Cassell Dictionary of Folklore*, David Pickering writes that the modern concept of the leprechaun is an old man with a strong sense of mischief who "delights in playing jokes upon mortals and features in countless humorous stories. In these a captured leprechaun often offers to grant a gullible human being three wishes or to reveal the whereabouts of treasure in return from being released." Actually the treasure is rarely secured because the elf is adept at diversion – suggesting to his captor that his cattle are breaking out of the field, his scythe is about to fall on his neck or a glass of fine *usce breatha* (gorse whiskey) awaits in the grass nearby.

The secret of catching a leprechaun, writes Hugh McGowan in *Leprechauns, Legends and Irish Tales*, is to creep upon him as he whistles at his work. Grab him tightly and never take your eyes off him. "He will pretend to be calm and unruffled, but all the time he is thinking how to escape. Hold him tight and stare at him hard because if you don't, he will vanish quicker than you can say 'bacon and cabbage.'"

In addition to making mischief, leprechauns make shoes. The belief that wee shoemakers have access to immense treasure is long established and reflected in a poem by nineteenth-century poet William Allingham:

Lay your ear close to the hill
Do you not catch the tiny clamor.
Busy click of an elfin hammer
Voice of the leprechaun singing shrill
As he merrily plies his trade?
He's a span
And a quarter in height,
Get him in sight, hold him tight,
And you're a made Man!

The celebrated Irish folklorist T. Crofton Croker tells of Michael O'Sullivan, an orphan lad, who spent all his nights reading by candlelight and by day selling turf from a handcart. One day coming across a leprechaun he asked where he could find gold. "Well, Michael, you're a lucky lad and no mistake. There's shocking rumors abroad that leprechauns is fierce and mean, and I'm going to squash that

thunderin' libel for all time." The little man led Michael to an abandoned fort and insisted he go in and help himself in the dark to coins from a bowl. The leprechaun warned Michael to get out before sunset. The lucky lad made the deadline just before the door slammed shut and went home with pockets full of gold coins. Michael lived well, bought a big house, filled it with books and never had to work. He never saw the leprechaun again, but every night when Michael emptied his pockets they were full of gold. The tale echoes the belief that leprechauns sometimes present strangers with *sparán na scillinge*, "purse of the shilling," the bottomless purse found in folklore everywhere.

The word "leprechaun" may derive from *Lu-chorpan*, "wee bodies," but according to the poet and paganist William Butler Yeats, the word comes from the old Irish *leith bhrógán*, the One Shoe Maker, since only one genuine leprechaun shoe ever seems to be found. But according to *The Treasury of Irish Folklore*, in a story by James Stephens a pair of shoes were made by a leprechaun for Seumas Beg. The leprechaun told the boy, "We grudge every minute spent making anything except shoes, for that is the proper work for a leprechaun. At night we go about the country into people's houses and we clip little pieces off their gold so little by little we get a crock of gold together so that if we're captured by menfolk we can ransom ourselves."

A few people have found shoes said to have been discarded by leprechauns. One was owned by nineteenth-century folklorist W.J. Patrick, who lived in the Mourne mountains of County Down. A picture of the shoe appeared in the *Mourne Observer* in the 1950's. And Yeats tells us that early in the nineteenth century a newspaper office in Tipperary displayed a single leprechaun-made shoe.

Some historians suggest that leprechauns originated as the Tuatha de Danaan, the Tribe of the goddess Danu, conquered by the Milesians and banished underground. The tribe shared the ambiguity of other Celtic figures who might have been gods or men, depending on whose account is believed. But although the word "leprechaun" derives only from the seventeenth century, as early as the eighth century legends existed of tiny folk with magical powers who made silver shoes that enabled wearers to walk on water.

Although usually depicted as amiable and carefree, leprechauns have a

dark side, according to Bob Curran. In *The Truth about the Leprechauns* he declares that they are not particularly good company and often selfish and miserly. He writes that although usually unseen, a leprechaun can sometimes be detected by a small whirlwind or cloud of dust, in which case old men doff their hats and women curtsy. If you throw your left shoe after the cloud, the leprechaun will be obliged to drop what he is carrying – which could be a bag of gold.

Curran also tells us that the wee creatures are reputed to be fine musicians, especially adept fiddlers and harpists. "Rory Dall O'Cahan, the composer credited with some of the most famous Irish melodies, including 'The Londonderry Air,' better known as 'Danny Boy,' reputedly heard it being played on a leprechaun's harp along the marshy banks of the Roe River in north Derry."

But the author cautions that extreme care must be taken by those who overhear leprechaun music. "The sprite may include some magic in the tune and the listener may find it impossible to resist dancing. Seeing that he has the dancer in his power, the leprechaun will increase the speed and tempo of the tune, making his captive leap and gambol faster and faster in time with the music. This he does for spite and mischief and some people have been known to die from exhaustion after performing the leprechaun's reel."

presage

by Dikki-Jo Mullen

ARIES 2004 — PISCES 2005

Visualize the web of a spider. Between the silvered strands lies open space, the void. A miniscule movement, perhaps a brush of a butterfly wing, a breath of air, or even the footstep of a faerie can set the whole web aquiver. Weaving and web motifs recur as central themes in numerous ancient legends. They remind us that human fate is part of a moving pattern. Stability is always fragile and transitory.

Astrology is the study of individual cosmic patterns that help the witch to understand the greater web of cosmic energies which surrounds us. It describes what we can cling to and what is going to shake the strands in the web of our own spirituality and destiny. By observing the themes and trends in the heavens above, a life of greater health, magic, love, beauty, and richness is assured.

Spring is ready to greet us and weave the web. The Sun reaches zero degrees of Aries on March 20, 2004 at 1:48 am EST. Saturn hovers in the sensitive water sign of Cancer, where it will remain all year. There can be strong karmic links that will both challenge and delight forming between those of widely different age groups. Uranus will also be in a water sign. This planet

of freedom and innovation spends the whole year in Pisces. Technology which will enhance health can be developed. Uranus moves in a mutual reception with Neptune in Aquarius. A mutual reception takes place when two planets are positioned in each other's ruling signs. (Neptune rules Pisces and Uranus rules Aquarius.) It's considered most fortuitous. Neptune in Aquarius accents unknown potentials within the human psyche. The mutual reception involving Uranus and Neptune allows each of us to make positive changes, to escape whatever we must, in order to move on.

Venus remains in Gemini an exceptionally long time, from April 3–August 7. This is worthy of note because the celestial love goddess usually stays less than a month in a single sign. In addition Venus presents us with a retrograde cycle mid-May to late June. The meaning of love itself, particularly regarding questions of commitment, is in a state of flux under this trend. Read all about how these and many more cosmic cycles will directly impact you in Presage. Consider the pages relating to your Moon and ascendant signs as well as the familiar Sun or birth sign for a more detailed astrological overview of the year to come.

ASTROLOGICAL KEYS

Signs of the Zodiac
Channels of Expression

ARIES: pioneer, leader, competitor
TAURUS: earthy, stable, practical
GEMINI: dual, lively, versatile
CANCER: protective, traditional
LEO: dramatic, flamboyant, warm
VIRGO: conscientious, analytical
LIBRA: refined, fair, sociable
SCORPIO: intense, secretive, ambitious
SAGITTARIUS: friendly, expansive
CAPRICORN: cautious, materialistic
AQUARIUS: inquisitive, unpredictable
PISCES: responsive, dependent, fanciful

Elements

FIRE: Aries, Leo, Sagittarius
EARTH: Taurus, Virgo, Capricorn
AIR: Gemini, Libra, Aquarius
WATER: Cancer, Scorpio, Pisces

Qualities

CARDINAL	FIXED	MUTABLE
Aries	Taurus	Gemini
Cancer	Leo	Virgo
Libra	Scorpio	Sagittarius
Capricorn	Aquarius	Pisces

CARDINAL signs mark the beginning of each new season — active.
FIXED signs represent the season at its height — steadfast.
MUTABLE signs herald a change of season — variable.

Celestial Bodies
Generating Energy of the Cosmos

Sun: birth sign, ego, identity
Moon: emotions, memories, personality
Mercury: communication, intellect, skills
Venus: love, pleasures, the fine arts
Mars: energy, challenges, sports
Jupiter: expansion, religion, happiness
Saturn: responsibility, maturity, realities
Uranus: originality, science, progress
Neptune: dreams, illusions, inspiration
Pluto: rebirth, renewal, resources

Glossary of Aspects

Conjunction: two planets within the same sign or less than 10 degrees apart, favorable or unfavorable according to the nature of the planets.

Sextile: a pleasant, harmonious aspect occurring when two planets are two signs or 60 degrees apart.

Square: a major negative effect resulting when planets are three signs from one another or 90 degrees apart.

Trine: planets four signs or 120 degrees apart, forming a positive and favorable influence.

Quincunx: a mildly negative aspect produced when planets are five signs or 150 degrees apart.

Opposition: a six sign or 180 degrees separation of planets generating positive or negative forces depending on the planets involved.

The Houses — Twelve Areas of Life

1st house: appearance, image, identity
2nd house: money, possessions, tools
3rd house: communications, siblings
4th house: family, domesticity, security
5th house: romance, creativity, children
6th house: daily routine, service, health

7th house: marriage, partnerships, union
8th house: passion, death, rebirth, soul
9th house: travel, philosophy, education
10th house: fame, achievement, mastery
11th house: goals, friends, high hopes
12th house: sacrifice, solitude, privacy

ECLIPSES

Eclipses always generate a certain mystique and sense of intrigue. The shadow of the heavenly body (usually the Sun or Moon) whose light is blocked, that is eclipsed, during an exact alignment with the Earth sweeps across the sky. This shadow obscures the glow of either the Sun or Moon for a time. As the light is extinguished, out of the momentary darkness, comes new growth. An eclipse is like an exclamation point combined with an element of surprise. It's exciting at the least and sometimes downright chaotic. The nodes of the Moon determine the occurrence and totality of eclipses which involve the Sun, Earth, and Moon. Long ago ritual magic was dedicated to these celestial events. The modern witch would do well to honor and heed the messages eclipses offer. Those eclipses which conjoin the north node of the Moon are thought to be more favorable than the eclipses conjunct the south node. When an eclipse is within three degrees of a planet in the birth chart it will stir the latent potentials of that planet. The most powerful impacts occur when the eclipse is within three days of the birthday, for this shows a conjunction with the natal Sun. Solar eclipses always occur at the New Moon with the Sun and Moon in the same sign. Lunar eclipses take place with the Full Moon as the Sun and Moon oppose each other positioned exactly across the zodiac. Unusual weather and significant world events can occur near the time of an eclipse. Don't force decisions or choices during an eclipse. It's best to pause and observe before acting.

April 19	Solar Eclipse in Aries, north node — partial
May 4	Lunar Eclipse in Scorpio, south node — total
October 13	Solar Eclipse in Libra, south node — partial
October 27	Lunar Eclipse in Taurus, north node — total

PLANETS IN RETROGRADE MOTION

When retrograde, a planet appears to be moving backwards — an optical illusion created by its rate of travel relative to Earth's motion. Illusion or not, the impact is one that changes all of the usual rules. Awareness of repeating patterns is important in making needed changes, for retrogrades mark times when a second chance is offered. It's wise to look at new perspectives and approach situations from an alternate vantage point. Consider the retrograde planet's rulership and influences to determine exactly how to do this.

Mercury turns retrograde more often than any other planet. For about three weeks three or four times a year it will delay travel, scramble communication, and bring back old acquaintances. Avoid making a move or beginning a new job or project while Mercury is retrograde, for the changes will have a lack of stability and permanence. Retrograde Mercury cycles are wonderful times to pursue past life regression and to visit museums or antique shops. Here are the upcoming Mercury cycles:

April 6 - April 30, 2004
in Taurus and Aries

August 9 - September 2, 2004
in Virgo and Leo

November 30 - December 20, 2004
in Sagittarius

Venus turns retrograde less frequently than any other planet. When this does take place it's best to be patient regarding matters of the heart. The tender feelings are prone to shift. Manage finances with discretion. It's not the time to risk an impulsive expenditure. A new slant on creative expression can develop while Venus is retrograde. True love wears an unfamiliar face. Venus will be retrograde in Gemini May 17–June 29, 2004.

ARIES

*The year ahead for those
born under the sign of the Ram*
March 21–April 20

Adventurous, impulsive, and active with a trademark straightforwardness, you always project a special warmth and charisma. Your ruler, Mars, hints at your warrior nature. Aries will stir up the status quo just to relieve the tedium of daily life. Your heroic and enterprising confidence is best understood in reflecting upon the mythological account of the brave cosmic Ram. When the zodiac was young he rescued the brother and sister Phrixus and Helle from wicked Ino.

At the vernal equinox you will make plans for travel. Mercury will move rapidly through your birth sign until All Fools' Day. You will lead discussions and win debates using clever repartee. A great capacity for problem solving is in evidence as your birthday approaches. Mars will influence your 3rd house through the week following Beltane. This promises a variety of important letters and phone calls. You will be juggling several projects and appointments simultaneously. Confirm plans with others to avoid confusion, and much can be accomplished.

The April 19 solar eclipse in your own sign of Aries heralds what you welcome most of all–an opportunity for growth and change. Prepare for an exciting year. Neptune will turn retrograde in the sector ruling friendships and group affiliations on May 18. Avoid those who indulge in negative habits. Double-check the agendas and priorities of organizations you are involved with. There's an emphasis on home and family life from late May through Midsummer Day. Mars will join Saturn in your 4th house at that time. Focus on deepening bonds with relatives. Attend to home maintenance and repair projects.

As summer passes you will experience a psychic connection with animal companions. Jupiter is strongly aspected in your 6th house. Fated circumstances could bring a new animal resident to your household by July 4. During the long, bright days of July through the week following Lammastide, Mars in Leo shines with a 5th house trine aspect. Vacations will be wonderful, and you can achieve a new level of expertise in a favorite sport. Romantic involvements during this cycle will be especially exciting, possibly changing your entire life. During August Mercury will join Jupiter in your health sector. Mars will follow. It's a wonderful cycle to overcome persistent maladies or poor health habits. Efforts to improve your health will meet with rewards as the month ends.

September 1-10 Mercury will retrograde into Leo. Long-standing communication problems with a child or romantic interest can be overcome. The last three weeks of September finds Venus in Leo adding affection and charm to your love sector. At the same time Venus is making a favorable trine to Pluto in Sagittarius, another friendly fire sign. The result of this is a deep sense of connectedness in romance. The celestial influences kindle true love near the autumnal equinox. The Full Moon on September 29 in Aries highlights your own talents and beauty in a special way. Perform an esbat ritual focused on attracting recognition and opportunity.

As October begins Mars, Mercury, Jupiter, and the Sun will all be in Libra, your opposing sign. A competitive mood is present. Listen to the suggestions of others. Compromises spell success now. The Libra eclipse of October 13 will bring the specifics into focus. By All Hallows Eve a new source of income could be offered. The October 27 eclipse in Taurus ushers in an emphasis on the financial sectors of your birth chart. Your values as well as philosophy concerning money are transforming. Throughout the first three weeks of November, Venus and Neptune aspects will bring a charming and attractive acquaintance into your social circle. Maintain a touch of reserve to make the best impression.

From Thanksgiving through Yuletide an abundance of water sign transits will make you especially aware of the afterlife. A message may come from someone who has passed on. Mercury retrograde during the first week of December favors enjoying a traditional holiday season. Honor what has been customary. The end of December ushers in an active time, for a stellium of planets in Sagittarius, including Venus, Mars, Mercury, and Pluto, supports your 9th house. It's a wonderful time to focus on various learning experiences or to travel to sacred sites on a spiritual pilgrimage. Philosophical discussions linked to rituals and spells with those more learned in the craft can deepen your own faith.

From January 1 through Candlemas, February 2, Mars remains in harmony. Your vitality will be good and the highest ideals will motivate you. Career ambitions develop during January. You'll want to contribute and achieve. Avoid involvement in job politics though. An opposition from transit Saturn to several planets in your 10th house shows some delicate situations existing among professional associates. It is wise to remain alert and cautious and all will be well.

Friends are genuinely a blessing during February, for Venus forms a sextile from the 11th house. Ask for advice or favors near Valentine's Day. March opens with an unaccustomed discretion. A strong 12th house includes Uranus and the Sun. There is much brewing within you that companions can't quite perceive. You will recognize the wisdom of keeping your own counsel. The last days of winter are a time to be especially patient and subtle regarding love. On March 6 Mercury enters your sign. Acquire books or educational audio and video tapes. Travel and languages are apropos topics for discussion and study. Plan to visit a sacred site.

HEALTH

The year begins with healing Jupiter retrograde in your 6th house of wellness, a trend which culminates on May 5. Use the early weeks of spring to correct any bad health habits. Strength and recovery are building. The April 19 eclipse in your own sign can bring some eyestrain. Splurge on an eye exam. Install the very best lighting in your home and work place. The companionship of a special animal can play an important part in your well being. This might mean physical exercise through, say, walking a dog. An animal friend's unconditional love and psychological support can ease stress.

LOVE

The very long passage of Venus through Gemini this year, from early April until after Lammastide, accents social contacts coming through neighbors or siblings. Practice writing the perfect love letter or poem. Communicating your feelings is significant if you are to successfully woo the perfect partner. Commuter travel can also cause romance to flourish. The last three weeks of September and the Yuletide season also bring favorable Venus angles and the promise of love.

SPIRITUALITY

Friends share important spiritual insights this year, for Neptune highlights the 11th house of fellowship. This inspiration peaks with the July 31 Full Moon. Devote extra time and care to the early harvest cycle at the Lammas sabbat this year. Corn and grain goddess images can be especially meaningful. Research recipes for home baked sabbat breads using a variety of grains. Consider the historical and mythological attributes of the various grains.

FINANCE

Relatives a generation older or younger might need some financial assistance. Saturn squares your Sun from the home and family sector the year long. The May 4 and October 27 eclipses both impact your finances. Prepare for changes in the status quo. The Hallowmas sabbat is an optimum time for prosperity magic.

TAURUS

The year ahead for those born under the sign of the Bull
April 21–May 21

A child of Venus, you enjoy fine garments and surroundings marked by comfort and beauty. But these sensual Taureans need stability and security. Don't let persistence and permanence become bullish inflexibility and stubbornness. It's important to recognize when change is needed and to adapt if you are to reach your ultimate potential. Bent upon charming Europa, Jupiter took the form of a white bull, Taurus. He lured her into mounting him, then rushed her away to Crete. Taurus has a way of getting what it wants.

With the vernal equinox Mars is just leaving your birth sign. A cycle of frantic activity and competition culminates. Welcome the spring by taking some time to revel in the peace and quiet of nature. Release old anger and anguish. Venus glides in conjunction with your Sun through April 2. A new love can brighten your life as the year begins. Develop creative ideas. On the eve of All Fools' Day Mercury touches the cusp of your birth sign where it will remain until it retrogrades back into Aries on April 12. This time span favors looking at a variety of options, especially regarding travel.

The remainder of April through May Eve finds both Venus and Mars in Gemini highlighting your 2nd house. It's a wonderful time to boost earning power through experimenting with creative ideas. Devotion to career promises deep satisfaction near Beltane, and a professional associate becomes a closer friend. A partner decides to upset the status quo near the lunar eclipse in your 7th house on May 4. You'll insist upon balance and justice. A Full Moon ritual devoted to those ideals would be effective.

On May 17 through the end of June Venus, your ruler, is retrograde in your money sector. Seek a bargain and enjoy all you have rather than longing for that which is costly. Be aware of old habits regarding money management. It's tempting to procrastinate just after your birthday. Say a blessing on your clocks and appointment calendar so that time doesn't get away from you. Don't arrive late for really important liaisons and other meetings. Reputation and image must be nurtured now.

July finds Mars and Mercury moving rapidly through your 4th house. You'll play host to visitors. Home improvements can be planned. Experiment with bold, bright colors. By Lammastide Mercury will join Jupiter in your sister earth sign of Virgo. Both will trine your Sun. It's a marvelous time to plan a vacation. Hobbies could lead to a new career direction. Children have much to teach you and can be a catalyst for change.

September finds Mars and the Sun joining the other Virgo transits. Athletic activities may develop into a genuine passion. A new competitive quality will develop. Romantic prospects build in interest during the days before the autumn equinox.

Just after the autumn equinox Jupiter changes signs, beginning a year-long passage through your 6th house. Health will take a turn for the better during the bright, crisp weeks of autumn. Animal companions are especially in tune with your needs now. The October 13 eclipse will bring the specifics into focus. From early October until just before Hallowmas Venus is well aspected. Enjoy exercise or spiritual healing sessions with a loved one. Accept invitations. An admirer is making a special effort to add to your happiness. October 27 a Full Moon eclipse in your birth sign adds sparkle and surprise. A turning point impacting your long-term future is due. Devote the sabbat to blessing changes and growth. Let an old door close.

Mercury and Pluto in your 8th house will quincunx Saturn in Cancer during November. Keep a positive mindset. Negative programming, especially about economic issues, can seem discouraging. Cope by seeking to understand the force of fate and destiny. Make the best of what is dealt to you. Research that which puzzles you. Knowledge will bring empowerment. Early December highlights legal matters. A confrontation or paperwork can be resolved by the 16th. Seasonal greetings will bring sentimental messages, for there are many water sign transits in the heavens. Others are emotional and sensitive. Be kind, offer sympathy.

After Yuletide relationships will enter a calmer phase. Others will be less demanding. With winter's onset the Capricorn Sun allows your best qualities to shine. You will be an example to others. From the week of January 10 until Candlemas Venus and Mercury will dance together through Capricorn. This brings a happy and friendly omen to your 9th house. Consider taking a winter vacation or enrolling in classes. Your writing and teaching abilities will be in top form. A favorable Mars aspect begins on February 7 and continues until winter ends. This marks a cycle of renewed energy. Your professional aspirations will bring a special sense of fulfillment by late March.

HEALTH

Early autumn promises a dramatic improvement in wellness, for benevolent Jupiter enters your 6th house of health on September 24. It will remain there through the remainder of the year. A double Venus pattern comes into play as the transit will be in Libra. Beauty has a real ability to heal now. A visit to a luxurious health spa would be rejuvenating. Crystals can also be extremely beneficial. Try wearing a moss agate or aventurine to draw a deep earthy vitality.

LOVE

The May 4 eclipse will rock your sector of relationships. Changes are brewing near your birthday regarding commitments. Welcome growth and new cycles in the lives of those you care most about. Retrograde Venus begins on May 17. Kindness and patience are of utmost importance. Be on guard and avoid repeating patterns. A past life connection with a loved one is being played out. Reflect on karmic connections in order to facilitate trust and acceptance. During October Venus comes to the rescue with a passage through your 5th house of pleasure and romance. A strongly aspected 7th house in early December brings success to a partner. Cement a bond by offering praise and support. Play the second fiddle well and Yuletide may find you settled happily with someone you truly care for.

SPIRITUALITY

Explore the history and spiritual attributes of herbs this spring. You are always talented in the garden, but an earthy Jupiter influence in Virgo during the first part of the year will allow you to connect with Mother Nature on a whole new level. Marjoram, rosemary, and mint would be wonderful plants to begin with. Prepare a dream pillow; dream imagery can bring a deeper spiritual insight regarding your purpose in life. Mystical Neptune holds court at the very top of your birth chart. You will find ways to bring a spiritual note into your career environment. The week of the Full Moon on July 31 will bring this pattern to a peak.

FINANCE

Venus will make an exceptionally long passage through Gemini, which links to your 2nd house of finances this year. The transit will span April 3–August 7. Overall, this will be good regarding cash flow and earning ability. You will be able to make purchases you've longed for, and it will be possible to use money to generate true enjoyment. However, while Venus is retrograde from mid-May to late June be cautious about over-extending. Compare prices and remember to budget. It may be wise to tear up credit cards if charges are mounting.

GEMINI

*The year ahead for those
born under the sign of the Twins*
May 22–June 21

Gemini illustrates the dual quality of the mind, of inner change and creativity accomplished through external interaction. Alert, versatile, and restless, life for Gemini people is always active on a variety of levels at the same time. Much is learned and accomplished through the medium of conversation. The Gemini Twins, Castor and Pollux, are the privileged and divine children of Leda and Jupiter. Lesser gods of earth, the pair are famed in myth for their devotion to each other.

From the vernal equinox until All Fools' Day your ruling planet Mercury will aspect Pluto favorably. The 11th house is involved. Disputes with a partner can be resolved through the mediation of mutual friends. During April your direction will have to be revamped as Mercury will turn retrograde. Be patient; success comes before Beltane. Venus will brighten your birth sign for a very long time this year, April 3–August 7. Develop creative potentials. Purchase an attractive journal and matching pen to record ideas. They're likely to be too good to let them fall by the wayside. Artistic endeavors of all kinds will flourish.

It's easy to be a bit abrupt during April and early May, for powerful Mars will be in conjunction with your Sun. Seek a constructive outlet for energy. Much can be accomplished if you don't give way to anger. Mid-May finds your 12th house accented. Replenish your vitality by taking time to rest and regroup. A very rapid

passage of your ruler, Mercury, through your own birth sign favors travel during June. Become focused on a project. You can complete it with aplomb near the time of the Gemini New Moon on June 17.

Midsummer Day finds Mars crossing the cusp of your 3rd house where it will remain through Lammas. A neighbor or sibling expresses strong opinions and makes suggestions. This accelerates July 4 when Mercury joins Mars in Leo. Promptly respond to calls and messages to enhance success. There is likely to be a series of impromptu short journeys during July. August finds Jupiter highlighted by other Virgo transits in your home and family sector. Opportunities to change living arrangements for the better are being presented. Do this before Mercury turns retrograde on August 9. During September interesting facts about your heritage will surface. Read old letters and diaries for clues.

October finds a stellium of planets gathering in your brother air sign of Libra and your 5th house. Romantic interludes are a source of genuine delight. A new hobby or form of creative expression can become very important to you. The eclipse on October 13 at the Libra New Moon will focus this delightful pattern. Wander to a solitary place on the eve of the Full Moon of October 27. Your 12th house is accented in an unusual way by the lunar eclipse pattern. Quiet reverie is a must. By the 31st you will be more social and extroverted again. Dress in costumed finery and circulate at All Hallows.

During November Mercury will begin a long transit through Sagittarius, your opposing sign. Listen to and learn from others. Suggestions which you resist at first can prove to be valuable in the end. A close companion may have multiple projects in progress. Discussion will dispel confusion. Don't worry, you will have an opportunity to influence the course of action at the Gemini Full Moon on November 26.

Mercury will be retrograde as December begins; it turns direct on the eve of Yule. At the same time Mars will be making a quincunx aspect in your health sector. Get enough rest and avoid those who are unwell in any way. Allow extra time for holiday travel and preparations. Everything will seem to be in slow motion. At the solstice the pattern shifts and you can expect a very active finale to the year. Uranus in Pisces is direct in your career sector as the New Year opens. It makes an ambitious square aspect to your Sun too. Freedom and adventure will characterize your choice of professional focus. You could experiment with a new type of job or acquire new technology to update the familiar working atmosphere. It's a wonderful year to study astrology in depth.

Just before Candlemas Mercury will enter Aquarius where it will move rapidly until just after Valentine's Day. This creates great harmony, for it will enhance the beneficial influence of Jupiter in Libra; you will be surrounded by air sign trines. Doorways of opportunity will open. Be ready to make changes. Old barriers will dissolve and you can prepare a climate of ease and wish fulfillment. It's almost as if Aladdin's magic lamp is handed to you. Seize upon opportunities which arise. The transit lasts a scant 17 days but will leave a beneficial afterglow if you make the best of it. As February ends a variety of mutable sign aspects create tension and motivation. You can gain in experience, although it's a busy and unsettled time. Your dedication will help others near the time of the Full Moon at midnight on February 23-24.

The last weeks of winter find Mars transiting your 8th house. This sector relates to the afterlife. You can perceive spirits wandering through the frozen mornings. Offer them comfort and you will be rewarded with a message about times to come. If it's difficult to release old anger, a study of your past lives can restore perspective. Keep control of your own finances. Another could be reckless with resources near March 5 or 18.

HEALTH

The weeks before your birthday can accent health needs, for the May 4 eclipse falls in your 6th house. Be sensitive to changes within your body and all will be well. Pluto, which rules your health sector, will complete its retrograde on August 30. Address any questionable health habits before then and your vitality will improve. Learn the art of Pranayama, or healing yoga breathing, during the autumn to further promote wellness and longevity. Jupiter, the celestial healer, begins a long passage through Libra, your brother air sign, on September 24. Fresh air, the wind, and breath can assume a new importance in the quest for perfect health.

LOVE

You will enjoy the company of Venus in your birth sign this year for an exceptionally long time, from April 3 until August 7. Learn from old experiences and use them as a foundation upon which to build future happiness. Your beauty and charm are magnetic now and you will hard to resist. Circulate. Plan or attend parties at Beltane and Lammastide.

SPIRITUALITY

Uranus, ruler of your 9th house of philosophy, is in Pisces. It will form squares and oppositions to mutable sign transits as well as your Sun will all year long. You might enjoy experimenting with new forms of meditation and spiritual expression. Too much ritual and formality will generate restlessness. Keep incantations short. The gods and goddesses are apt to respond to humor and novelty now. A light heart sings a sweet song.

FINANCE

Saturn in Cancer describes your earning ability now. It's very important to be reliable and prompt. Keep close track of receipts and what is owed to you. Job skills might have to be updated. Be aware that if you change jobs, time and special effort may be required to return to your customary income. When Jupiter moves into Libra, shortly after the autumn equinox, you will experience an enhanced lifestyle. At the same time continue to manage money carefully and avoid waste. Saturn watches from the shadows in a square aspect and might pounce upon those who speculate unwisely.

CANCER

*The year ahead for those
born under the sign of the Crab*
June 22–July 23

Cancer, as the emblematic Crab hints, tends to be self contained. There is tremendous subjectivity, and the universe is interpreted in relation to personal perceptions. Though Moon children love deeply, they tend to keep the inner heart sheltered. The devoted Crab sacrificed itself to bite Hercules in the heel as he fought Hydra. In gratitude, Juno placed the lifeless shell among the stars where it sparkles; forever immortal, remote, and lovely.

With the spring Mars begins a passage through your 12th house. There may be some unvoiced anxiety or frustration to deal with. A friendly sextile from Venus in the 11th house shows that a companion could offer sympathy and help by All Fools' Day. During April, Aries transits in your career sector will square challenging Saturn. Saturn is the heavenly heavyweight and it is square in the middle of a two-year passage through your birth sign. Learn from disappointments and delays, then plod ahead patiently. Saturn's message is one of rewards for a job well done. It's strictly business before pleasure now.

Prepare a May Eve ritual to extend love and appreciation to coworkers. A sage smudge would do wonders if used to bless the work place. On May 7 Mars joins Saturn in your sign. It's very important not to give way to anger or recklessness. Keep trying. Rewards go to the determined and consistent ones. Rest and good humor are a must right now. Just after Midsummer Day

Mercury's energy replaces the Mars transit. Suddenly it will be easier to solve problems. Travel, especially by water, would be healing. A new perspective regarding challenging situations develops from the end of June through the July 4 holiday weekend. The New Moon in your sign on July 17 favors a fresh start.

The end of July brings Mercury and Jupiter in Virgo into a favorable double sextile aspect involving your 3rd house. This is good for talking through problems and finding answers. Honesty and ethical behavior provide the standards for success. Be a good listener. During the week following Lammas Venus will approach the Cancer cusp and begin a happy transit through your birth sign. An appreciation of your personal heritage comes during August and early September. Relationships will be more steady and satisfying from September 10 through the fall equinox as Mercury, Mars, Jupiter, and the Sun will all be in Virgo. The Virgo New Moon on September 14 focuses the nourishing potential of this grouping. Practical study, conversations, and short outings are all catalysts for progress. People and places in your immediate surroundings assume a deeper significance.

On September 24 Jupiter begins a year-long transit through your home and family sector. Real estate transactions should be profitable. The accomplishments of a family member will bring you joy. The Full Moon in Aries, your 10th house, on September 28 foreshadows trends to come. During October cardinal sign transits can make it tricky to balance family life with professional goals. Reflect at the New Moon Eclipse on October 13. Resolve to understand what isn't working and why. It's an optimum time to perform a space clearing ritual or house blessing. October will end on a progressive, happy note. Mercury's entry into Scorpio on October 15 completes a grand trine in water linking the best that Saturn in Cancer and Uranus in Pisces have to offer. Confidence and security are building. Astrology and other types of metaphysical counseling are especially helpful in the days before Halloween. A walk near the shore would be especially uplifting during an afternoon at the end of October.

November opens with some idle chatter among coworkers caused by Sagittarius transits forming tense aspects in the 6th house. Take gossip with the proverbial grain of salt. On November 11 Mars moves into Scorpio. The weeks from mid-November through Yule will be bright and productive. This trend brings the very best potentials of Saturn's long-term influence in your birth sign to the fore. Relationships with males as well as elders and authority figures will improve. Vitality and strength will be enhanced. Previous disappointments no longer seem so hard to accept. The Full Moon in Cancer on December 26 brings new insight into your own psyche. The lunation is in mutual reception with Saturn, which is most auspicious. A new talent can be developed in the days to come.

As 2005 begins Venus will conjoin Pluto in Sagittarius, underscoring the role of animal companions. A new cat or other familiar can appear. During the last half of January Capricorn oppositions could make it important to attend to a legal matter. Allow a companion to make suggestions and lead the way. Subtle nuances are afoot near Candlemas. Read between the lines and do some research. Mysteries can be solved. Clues are present, for your 8th house holds three planets and the Sun. From February 7 through the end of winter a stimulating and competitive mood is present. Mars will oppose your Sun and stimulate Saturn's influence. Much is expected of you. Avoid confrontations and don't seek too many favors. Maintaining a calm independence is best. A lovely trine from Venus in Pisces moves into play after February 27. Spiritual and well educated companions uplift you. Romantic contacts may be encountered at meditation circles or in classes. A creative project brings fulfillment at the New Moon in Pisces on March 10.

HEALTH
The ingestion of foods and the stomach are especially linked to your birth sign. Moon children are especially prone to indigestion, heartburn, and unstable weight. With Mars and Saturn, combined in a vortex in your sign during May and June, it's important to select light and healthy meals. Keep papaya enzyme tablets or fresh papaya on hand as a home remedy to soothe the tummy. Eat rich and spicy foods in small servings only at this time.

LOVE
Friendly Uranus in your sister water sign of Pisces is adding sparkle and surprises. This promises interesting new possibilities. Travel, study, or attending spiritual groups can be catalysts for making contacts. Venus will compliment Uranus August 8–September 5, November 22–December 15, and February 27–March 19. Mutual friends can initiate introductions which will prove to be important. Initiate a discussion about compatibility in astrology charts to reach out to an attractive new prospect.

SPIRITUALITY
Visionary Neptune rules your spiritual sector. Dreams can bring significant messages from higher consciousness. Begin to keep a dream journal. Learn about the various categories of dreams, including lucid dreams. While drifting into sleep ask for guidance. Past lives can be revisited in your dream time close to the Full Moon each month. In esoteric astrology the Moon links to the emotional rememberings of the soul. Past life images can become a valuable tool to aid in coping with present day experiences.

FINANCE
Saturn will conjoin your Sun all year, and the Sun rules your 2nd house of finances. It's important to work hard and to be self reliant. A conservative work ethic really will prove rewarding. You have a natural affinity for antiques and collectibles. Trades and purchases of these can add to your income. A much younger or older person will be grateful for your financial assistance. Enjoy what you have and forget about what is temporarily too costly. Do not acquire more debt this year.

LEO

The year ahead for those
born under the sign of the Lion
July 24–August 23

The noble Lion has had to endure stereotyping. Yes, the characteristic description of proud, creative, and dramatic with a noble dignity does apply to Leo. However, on a deeper level this birth sign is about self awareness. The point is to move up the evolutionary spiral to a higher level. The Nemean lion came originally from above to confront Hercules. The star Regulus, emblem of a royal soul, marks the shining heart of that Lion in the sky.

As the spring stirs you'll seek wider intellectual horizons. Mercury moves through your 9th house until early April. Purchase books and consider attending classes or arranging an informative journey. Friends can seem quite opinionated through Beltane. Mars will be in your 11th house in opposition to Pluto. Help a comrade to direct anger in a constructive way. Choose associates with discretion.

On May 4 Jupiter turns direct in your financial sector. Old debts are resolved, and situations regarding income improve. Through May 20 the Sun will brighten your 10th house of fame and fortune. You'll be highly visible at work and make an impression on influential individuals. During the last half of May Neptune will begin a retrograde pattern in opposition to you. Don't repeat counterproductive patterns in relationships or legal matters. Honesty and credibility will prove to be especially precious during the next few months. As Midsummer Day approaches invitations come

your way. A casual acquaintance could misunderstand your intentions. Clarify expressions of love as opposed to friendship.

June 23 finds fiery Mars entering your sign of Leo where it will remain through the week following Lammastide. Since you are a Sun-ruled fire sign, this Martian transit augurs an active summer. Initiate projects. Exercise can be especially satisfying. An old obstacle can be eliminated during the last week of July when Mars will trine Pluto.

On August 7 Venus will enter your 12th house. A month-long cycle begins during which you'll deeply appreciate reverie and solitude. Great creative inspiration can develop while you're alone. Keep a journal to preserve your notes and sketches for future reference. Mercury will retrograde back into Leo from August 24–September 9. Thoughts come together with new depth and power then. A second chance at a project or job is offered. It will become easier to socialize when Venus enters Leo on September 6. Through the autumn equinox your charming demeanor will attract both love and money. As September ends, a stellium of Libra planets including Jupiter, Mars, Mercury, and the Sun will highlight your communication sector. Make calls, arrange meetings, and attend to correspondence. You can suddenly feel very proud of the accomplishments of a sibling. The October 13 Libra eclipse will underscore the full potentials of this trend.

During the two weeks before Samhain a past life recollection can slip into your dreamtime. Scenes near the waterfront are likely to be a part of this, for Uranus will be retrograde in Pisces, the home of your natal 8th house. This is the gate through which we view other lives in the birth chart. Celebrate Halloween at home. With Mercury conjunct the Sun in your sector of residence and family, it's a perfect time to do a house blessing. The Tarot cards have a message about domestic matters.

From mid-November through Yule Mars will agitate your home and real estate sector. Plan to redecorate or repair your dwelling by the year's end. Appreciate and honor it–don't let a groundless, vague dissatisfaction invade your haven. 2005 begins with an emphasis on health and fitness. The New Moon on January 10 in Capricorn will oppose Saturn. The relationship between stress, your psyche, the wholesomeness of your employment conditions, and your physical health will be very apparent. The Full Moon at the end of January falls in your sign. It will be easier to understand how to do what's best for yourself as the month ends. Be cautious about following the advice of others verbatim. One who means well is apt to be mistaken.

From Candlemas through Valentine's Day charming and eloquent companions go out of their way to include you in plans. A telepathic exchange can occur, providing a deeper glimpse into the heart and mind of a partner. The last two weeks of February accent financial strategies. The combined influences of Mercury, the Sun, and Uranus in Pisces in a quincunx aspect to Leo suggest that sources of security can be shifting. Gather information and diversify regarding financial planning. When Venus joins the pattern at the end of February, monetary situations will be assured of greater success. From March 5 through the final days of winter beneficial aspects from Mercury and Pluto in the other two fire signs bring an ease in making plans. Your wit and vocabulary will open doors and win admiration.

HEALTH

The relationship between a positive state of mind, faith, and dedication to your health will be very apparent this year. Saturn, an important health indicator, is currently moving through the 12th house, the sector of self-undoing. The idea of being your own best friend in developing a healthy lifestyle must be embraced. During the month preceding your birthday pay heed to an inner voice warning of danger. Seafood, including seaweed and sea salt, has multiple trace minerals that would be especially healing at present. Demands made by others can be rather draining. Replenish your energy by periodically spending a few quiet moments alone.

LOVE

A long Venus passage in your 11th house in Gemini shows that friends and lovers can change roles. Get to know those whom you admire better from early April until your birthday. A sense of humor and the art of pleasant conversation will be the keys to entering a new social circle then. When Venus enters Leo in September warm feelings are shared with a special someone and love becomes more stable. Elusive and mystical Neptune in your commitment sector could bring an artistic or spiritual partner your way. Gently but resolutely release any addictive loves. Addictive loves are those which seem compelling but which bring only sorrow and frustration, not peace and nurture.

SPIRITUALITY

The Sun, your ruler, is the source of all life on Earth. The Sun sign in the horoscope is the single most important factor to consider in an astrological reading. This is a wonderful year to explore different types of Sun worship. Begin by meditating regularly on sunrises and sunsets. Then make it a habit to feel the life-giving, antiseptic powers of the full spectrum light near high noon. Research solar deities from different mystical traditions. Might the Sun literally be watching over the destiny of Earth? The New Moon in Leo on August 15 can bring some answers.

FINANCE

Think about perfecting your salable job skills in order to boost earning potential as the new year begins. Generous Jupiter, the celestial wealth indicator, is transiting your 2nd house of earned income and cash flow from spring until just after the autumn equinox. This will present opportunities which, if properly developed, can enhance future security. Since analytical Virgo is involved in this pattern, it makes sense to keep very neat and complete financial records. Remember not to become anxious regarding financial situations. It wastes time and energy. After all, money is only of value for the good it brings about, not for its own sake.

VIRGO

The year ahead for those
born under the sign of the Virgin
August 24–September 23

Virgo enjoys a traditional link to ritual magic. Recognition of the specific spirits linked to detailed phenomena is suited to Virgo's meticulous side. Thoughtful and discriminating are traits associated with the Virgin, the second of the Mercury-ruled signs. Tied to communication, particularly fluency with the written word, Virgo tends to be a productive writer. Many successful authors and teachers share this birth sign.

Spring begins with Venus in Taurus through All Fools' Day, creating a harmonious trine in earth signs. Your 9th house is favored. Artwork and imported items of all types will bring pleasure. Travel is a catalyst for both profit and friendship. During April two Gemini transits accent your fame and fortune sector. You'll be ambitious and compete enthusiastically to attain success. Patience is a must, though, for Mercury will turn retrograde on April 6. Throughout the remainder of the month be cheerful while you reconnect, reconsider, revamp, and reflect. On May Eve a favorable Saturn aspect to Jupiter in your sign brings rewards. As May progresses benevolent Jupiter completes its retrograde and moves rapidly forward in your Sun sign through your birthday. A cycle of great blessings and opportunity unfolds. Mid-May through early June brings a Mercury transit through Taurus which will generate some worthwhile ideas and options. Be proactive.

During the June days leading up to the summer solstice, a Mars sextile generates active and interesting social contacts. A dynamic friend is an inspiration. Focus on forming clear goals. The sector of hopes and wishes is accented through Midsummer Day. Don't lose focus or shift priorities. Dissipating precious energy could end in frustration. July finds your 12th house emphasized. You'll enjoy the peace and solitude of nature. Performing a random act of kindness for one who is ill or disadvantaged will bring a personal blessing.

Meditate on self awareness and personal responsibility at Lammas. By August 10 the mood shifts. Forceful Mars begins a transit that day and will move toward a conjunction with Jupiter in Virgo. Adventure and a new assertiveness will characterize your approach toward life in general. Simultaneously Mercury will turn retrograde. This creates a complicated sensation of applying the gas and the brakes at the same time. Keep anger in check, be flexible, and August will be a memorable month. On September 2 Mercury will turn direct. The Sun will join Mars and Jupiter in your sign and all blockages will evaporate. The three weeks preceding Mabon will be marvelous for healing on all levels. Your strength and enthusiasm are at a peak; others look to you for leadership. October's eclipse pattern accents finances. A source of income could change for you or a partner. At the same time you will have a sudden desire to make major purchases. Focus on prosperity rituals at All Hallows. A good influence from generous Jupiter will start to strengthen, bringing improved financial prospects.

November finds unpredictable Uranus completing a long retrograde through your relationship sector. Changes you've sensed coming in a partnership will start to manifest. Respect another's right of choice and individuality. Have a back-up plan in place if someone you've depended upon shows a tendency to be unreliable. Relationships are changing, but change is another word for growth. To change often is to grow much. December finds retrograde Mercury joining Pluto and the Sun in Sagittarius, highlighting home and family life. Don't move your residence now. Instead clean and organize in preparation for Yule. A Feng Shui treatment would be helpful. At the solstice Mercury is direct again, and the domestic situation becomes more settled. Relatives will be more relaxed as New Year's Eve approaches.

January 2005 opens with Mars joining three other planets in Sagittarius. Home and family issues must be addressed again. Redecorate and repair your home. A residential move can come about by the month's end. The New Moon on January 10 in Capricorn marks the start of a happy time. Venus will enter your 5th house of love and pleasure. A relationship, hobbies, and creative projects add to your happiness as the month ends. Up to Candlemas there is more time to do what you enjoy most. February begins with an accent on health and fitness. The Full Moon on the 23rd in your sign brings new insight into your own physical and emotional health perspectives. Make a record of a dream linked to health conditions. It will prove to be quite significant as the month ends.

A favorable Mars aspect enables you to shine against all competitors during March. Perfect and enjoy winter sports. Physical activity helps you to cope with complex people, for Venus, Uranus, and the Sun will all oppose you. Tolerance and humor are a must in approaching intimate relationships successfully.

HEALTH

A helpful mutual reception involving Uranus, ruler of your 6th house of health, and Neptune brings you into contact with the right people and circumstances to facilitate wellness. Experiment with alternative health techniques such as massage, yoga, and affirmations. Take reasonable care around those who are ill. Because of a long lasting Uranus opposition, a flu or other type of contagious bug could affect you. Step back from those who are depressing you or are perhaps psychologically draining. A psychic vampire must be avoided. Perform a simple but effective psychic self defense rite against such individuals by carrying a small packet of salt on your

person when you encounter them. Don't make eye contact or engage in pointless conversation.

LOVE

Venus will remain in your 10th house for a very long time this year, from April until August. It will strongly aspect Uranus which is in your 7th house of relationships. Prepare to balance love and relationships with the pleasure that dedication to your career brings. If you are fancy free, a new romantic interest can develop through your professional circle before your birthday. October and January both find Venus making wonderful aspects while transiting Earth signs. Circulate and be receptive to love then. Purchase a bouquet of bright flowers to welcome the goddess and her gifts.

SPIRITUALITY

Explore different spiritual traditions this year. Jupiter has a link to philosophical expansion, and it will remain in your birth sign through the autumn equinox. Combine a variety of beliefs in a way that reflects your own perception of the Lord and Lady. Protect your home by tracing some Pennsylvania Dutch hex symbols and painting them in bright colors while doing a positive visualization. A journey to a sacred site, perhaps combined with a hiking and camping expedition, could also provide an awakening.

FINANCE

Jupiter will enter your 2nd house of finance on September 24. Wait until then to take any risks. Early in the year a combination of mutable aspects will tempt you to overextend. There is a promise of abundance during the spring and summer seasons, yet you might yearn for more and not fully appreciate the bird in hand. This trend will peak at the summer solstice. Offer a word of gratitude during the summer season and focus on contentment. A peridot would be a wonderful gemstone for a prosperity talisman. Sales and promotional activities of various types can significantly add to your income all year. Bartering and bargain-hunting also prove worthwhile.

LIBRA
*The year ahead for those
born under the sign of the Scales*
September 24–October 23

The balance of the Scales illustrates turning points. Poised gracefully at the beginning of the harvest season and the gateway to winter, Libra suggests transitions and is all about measuring relationships. Art, partnerships and justice are linked to this sign and show that sharing in the most desirable way means everything to Librans. Thoth held the scales to weigh the human heart against the feather of Maat. The heart must be light enough to enjoy the afterlife.

Spring begins with both Mercury and Saturn making hard aspects to your Sun. It can be a little difficult to concentrate. Follow a schedule combined with positive affirmations. Ask others to rephrase if the meaning of their words aren't clear. This is especially true if you're asking about instructions. April finds both Venus and Mars in your brother air sign of Gemini. This is extremely favorable. Travel and study should both be very rewarding. Your energy level will be high and a new sense of optimism develops. The Full Moon in your own sign of Libra on April 5 brings a heightened awareness of potentials for the year to come. Perform some wind magic that night. Allow the breezes to waft around you as you gaze upward at the moon. A vision might come or a spirit message.

The eclipse of April 19 augurs changes in relationships. Be receptive to new options. During the first half of May, Mercury and Saturn create some friction. Use diplomacy in arguments. It may be wise to remain silent if angry. During the last half of May through most of June, Venus, your ruler, will be retrograde. Don't be concerned if you find you need extra rest and if there are delays. A second chance occurs at a lost love or an old job. However, don't be surprised if the old patterns repeat. Be forgiving if others display poor manners or dress inappropriately. Allow light and casual friendship to replace depth in love through Midsummer Day.

June and July find a variety of Cancer transits passing through your 10th house. Mars followed by Mercury and the Sun will join Saturn in that part of your horoscope. This accents career as well as fame and reputation. Competitors can be a source of inspiration; stay informed about new developments in your field of expertise. Career-related study or travel is worthwhile. Take time to release stress and overcome anxiety, though. During the weeks before and following Lammastide, Venus will complete an opposition to Pluto. Old resentments will melt away. People you were disappointed in before are growing and moving on. The healing power of love and forgiveness will be very apparent. On August 9 Mercury turns retrograde in Virgo. This conjoins other transits, including Jupiter in your 12th house. You will feel the need to withdraw and reflect.

As September begins, Mercury and Venus in Leo will make beneficial aspects in your 11th house. Friends are helpful and interesting. You will discuss projects for the future. Community activities, including politics, can be appealing. Just after the autumn equinox Mars and Mercury will enter your birth sign. Your vitality and enthusiasm will be especially high through November 10. Take extra care not to seem too forceful, as the Mars transit will square Saturn. This can generate an argumentative pattern. However, you can accomplish much if you explore constructive avenues of action. The Libra eclipse on October 13 marks an important point in this significant cycle. Celebrate All Hallows with some physical activity. Honor the old gods through dance. Connect with Hecate by taking a long walk. Be certain to stop and meditate at at her sacred place, a crossroads. Leave her a token before moving on.

Jupiter begins a once in 12-year passage through your sign near your birthday. By November the impacts of this potent year-long transit will start to become apparent. You are anxious to expand and explore. Your sphere of opportunity is about to increase. Growth on many levels is in progress. Until November 22 charming Venus dances hand in hand, conjunct with Jupiter in Libra. Neptune in Aquarius will trine the lovely duo. You can expect one of the most beneficial and memorable of months ever. Love will have a mystical and spiritual quality. Your creative ideas and charming persona will open many doors. A bit of a financial windfall turns up as well.

At Thanksgiving Sagittarius transits highlight your 3rd house. Commuter-length journeys are important. A neighbor could issue an interesting invitation. Current events will be of great interest. Subscribe to magazines and newspapers. While preparing for Yule, stay aware of your budget. Mars and Venus will be in your financial sector making it tempting to overspend. On the year's shortest day Mercury turns direct and confusion is replaced by clarity. Making plans is easier now.

Creating a comfortable home environment is a priority during January. There is an emphasis on family life and real estate. The New Moon in your 4th house on January 10 will bring out the specifics. Since this lunation will oppose Saturn in your career sector, you might either work at home or choose between family life and professional ambitions. On the eve of Candlemas, Mercury and the Sun come to the rescue, as they will move into Aquarius. Venus follows shortly afterward. A time of love and leisure begins. Expect an especially happy Valentine's Day. February finds your intuition at its best, for these Aquarian planets activate Neptune. Color and sound provide a background for expanding awareness and healing all month.

March finds a grand cardinal cross in effect. Much is expected of you. Protect yourself from winter's chill with warm garments and nutritious foods. The last three weeks of winter will be exciting but extremely hectic. Don't become overwhelmed. Stay centered with daily sessions of relaxation techniques.

HEALTH

All year Uranus will impact your 6th house of health. Because it is in mutual reception with Neptune you should respond well to health programs and treatments. Friends can offer valuable suggestions concerning health. The entry of Jupiter into your sign near your birthday will bode well. March can bring added pressures and you must make time to care for your body in late winter. Honor it as a temple of the spirit.

LOVE

Venus makes a long passage through your brother sign of Gemini from April—August this year. It will trine both your Libra Sun and transit Neptune in Aquarius to create a grand trine in air signs. There will be an ease regarding love then. Frlendships and more serious relationships touch other areas of your life. Don't make a commitment while Venus is retrograde from May 17—June 29. You may change your mind.

SPIRITUALITY

You always have an artistic bent. This year creative expression can be a catalyst for spiritual awakening. In May and June Venus will influence your 9th house of the higher mind. Explore different forms of sacred symbols to attain closer attunement with the divine mysteries.

FINANCE

The May 4 eclipse will fall in your 2nd house of personal earnings. The October 27 eclipse will impact the earnings of partners as well as investments, taxes and insurance. This will promise changes in your sources of income. Maximize personal gain by awareness of changes in the economy. In late September Jupiter, the traditional wealth indicator, will enter your birth sign for an entire year. A turn for the better in your fortune is likely. Perform prosperity rituals at both of the eclipses as well as at the autumn equinox to put favorable financial potentials into motion.

SCORPIO

*The year ahead for those
born under the sign of the Scorpion*
October 24–November 22

Subtle and mysterious, the Scorpion smiles at its popular association with passion and the afterlife because there is so much more beneath the surface. These themes are actually Scorpio's way of coping with isolation while experiencing a deeper level of existence. Healing from the consequences of possessive desire is an important part of Scorpio's life mission. Orion, the huntsman, was blinded upon insulting the beautiful Merope. The Scorpion proved that Orion was truly a fool by dealing a fatal sting after the hunter regained his sight and boasted that he could slay any creature.

Spring awakens with Venus facing you in an opposition. Others have a different viewpoint regarding love. Communicate. You'll prevail if you respect the perspectives of those you are intimate with. Through Beltane Mars will be in your 8th house. There is much exploring and probing in progress. It's an optimum time to undergo past life regression. Vitality may wane during April for Mercury will retrograde into your health sector. Focus on developing the best health habits and all will be well when the retrograde is complete on April 30. Devote the May Eve sabbat ritual to health and fitness blessings.

Prepare for some excitement near the May 4 total lunar eclipse in your sign. A residential or career move may be in progress. Be flexible. A favorable Moon–Saturn aspect to the eclipse promises help from those in positions of power and authority. The remainder of May through the summer solstice finds Mars in a supportive position as it moves through Cancer, your sister water sign. A journey, particularly one involving water, is a catalyst for growth and opportunity then. Healing is likely to occur during meditation and worship. From the solstice through the Independence Day weekend a strong Mercury aspect allows you to assimilate new ideas and make wise decisions.

The last three weeks of July Leo transits, including Mars, Mercury, and the Sun, gather in your career sector. Extra recognition is coming your way. Demonstrate your capabilities in situations which promise to facilitate advancement. The trend continues through Lammas. On August 7 Venus moves into Cancer, promoting relaxation and love through early September. Leisure travel will be beneficial, perhaps putting you in touch with a promising financial opportunity. On September 10 Mercury joins other planets in Virgo where it will highlight your 11th house. Devote the weeks before the autumn equinox to making a list of goals and deciding about political and community involvement. A bright, talented friend can provide inspiration and happiness before September ends.

New appreciation of the peace and freedom of solitude develops as October begins, for Jupiter, the Sun, Mercury, and Mars will form a stellium in Libra, your 12th house. Answers and inspiration come from within now. Perform an anonymous act of charity or kindness and a deep sense of satisfaction will develop by All Hallows. Consider travel on or shortly after Halloween. Mercury will be moving rapidly through your sign, and you would benefit from a change of scene.

The weeks following your birthday hold great romantic potential. Venus enters your sign by Thanksgiving where it conjoins your Sun through Yule. A flurry of invitations, love tokens, and other pleasures will make the cold, dark days a time of happiness. From mid-November until just before New Year's Eve, Mars will fly through Scorpio. You'll be enthused and motivated. 2004 will conclude on a very upbeat note.

Many worthwhile projects will be in the works.

2005 begins with Mercury, Pluto, and other transits in your sector of money and possessions. Thoughts tilt toward financial planning. Be versatile and creative in applying your job skills; earning ability will blossom. At the New Moon on January 10 the mood shifts. Playful sextile aspects will begin to stir with Capricorn transits touching your 3rd house. Wry, subtle humor will appeal. Send a clever greeting card to a friend (or enemy). Break work into small segments, working on several projects at once, to alleviate boredom.

Perform a house blessing or create other family-oriented charms at Candlemas. Psychic bonds between parents and children strengthen. Neptune in Aquarius will be met by Mercury and the Sun in your 4th house of heritage and residence as February begins. Dream analysis provides a key to better understand relatives or make decisions linked to housing. Venus will brighten the situation further when it changes signs on February 2. The rest of the month is excellent for decorating, entertaining, or even seeking a new residence. Near Valentine's Day you will especially cherish your home.

March will sparkle with romantic possibilities. Uranus in Pisces has been hovering expectantly in your love and pleasure sector all year. As winter wanes Venus and the Sun will conjoin Uranus, awakening its full potential. The New Moon on March 10 will focus the specifics of this trend. An existing relationship moves to a new level. If you're single and seeking, a charming and unusual new friend wins your heart. This trend is also very artistically inclined. If you focus your attention on creativity March can mark a time of building admiration and recognition.

HEALTH

Mars rules your health sector. The red planet ties in with energy, light, and heat. Sunlight carries tremendous health-giving and antiseptic properties. Bask in the healing rays of full spectrum light to recharge both your body and soul (avoiding the dangerous rays of midday, of course). Be aware of how the quality of light in your home or workplace is affecting you and adjust it until it is ideal. You will be amazed at how proper lighting can enhance your well-being. Perform health rituals and meditations by the light of a favorite lamp, lantern, or specialty candle.

LOVE

Recognize how friendship can be a catalyst for love this year. Accept invitations to meet friends. Sociable Uranus is in your 5th house of romance. This can bring a delightful series of new contacts. However, Uranus adores freedom, so allow the one you admire to make choices and express individuality if you want to succeed in love this year. Since Uranus is trine your Sun you can expect great happiness to be accompanied by change regarding the tender passions. A hobby shared with others can also invite a closer intimacy. Attend a conference of coin or stamp collectors, or exchange ideas about garden design.

SPIRITUALITY

Solemn Saturn in Cancer is transiting your 9th house of higher thought all year. Traditional holiday observances will help you connect with the deeper meaning of life. Ask elders for spiritual guidance. Delve into your family's heritage for more answers. Set aside a corner of the home or backyard to create a personal altar. Decorate it with a familiar keepsake. Perform a rite at the Full Moon on December 26 honoring a tradition which touches your heart. A great depth of spiritual understanding will follow.

FINANCE

Congratulate friends on their financial successes through the autumn equinox. A favorable Jupiter in your 11th house during the first part of the year shows that they might share some of the bounty with you. From early November until early January Mercury will transit your 2nd house of finance. Extra work, accessing new information, and travel can all be beneficial to your cash flow at that time.

SAGITTARIUS

*The year ahead for those
born under the sign of the Archer*
November 23–December 21

Ruled by Jupiter, the largest and most generous of planets, Sagittarius is linked to abundance and expansion. Forever galloping onward, questing for eternal values, you approach life as a great adventure dedicated to exploring unchartered realms. You can be intolerant of the mundane. Use diplomacy as you seek to uplift others on a daily basis, and you'll be loved and respected as a role model. Chiron, the wise Sagittarian Centaur, taught the sons of the elite and the divine. Achilles and the great physician Aesculapius were two of his famous students.

There's time to play–and probably win–a favorite game as spring begins. Through the end of March Mercury and the Sun highlight your sector of recreation and pleasure. A letter or phone call could mark the beginning of an intriguing romance. The Aries eclipse of April 19 brings an important development linked to this trend. Prepare for a change of heart. All of these trends highlight the 5th house, so March and April will mark a highly creative cycle. Beltane should be observed in peace and privacy. The May 4 eclipse, falling in your 12th house, will replenish your energies if you withdraw and reflect. Venus will turn retrograde in Gemini, your opposing sign, in mid-May. An old flame can be rekindled or a lost love found. Go slowly, however. There can be some complex relationship situations unfolding as the transit will form a challenging Pluto aspect. Resist the urge

to remake another; a power struggle could become a tempest. Use humor and good listening skills in dealing with others through the summer solstice. The Full Moon in your sign on June 3 will usher in a four-week cycle of significance regarding relationships and obligations of all kinds.

July brings an energizing trine from Mars in Leo, your brother fire sign. This will impact your 9th house. Travel and study will be important. You want to win every competition, and the hottest, brightest days of summer will bring you victory. From July 4–24 Mercury will join Mars in this triumphant dance. Your cleverness and eloquence enable you to find the quickest route to fulfillment. At Lammas perform some fame and fortune magic.

During August, the 10th house of career will be activated by several Virgo planets, including Jupiter. You'll experience renewed ambition and dedication. If you've been trying to develop a career, a breakthrough may come. Promote your image and display your talents now. At the same time an opposition to Uranus can bring some sudden meetings and partings. An electric quality pervades your professional sphere. September will continue to be hectic because Mars will be in Virgo, adding to the force of angular mutable patterns.

After the autumn equinox a more relaxed cycle starts. The Sun and Jupiter will sextile your sign from the 11th house. At the same time Venus in Leo trines Pluto in Sagittarius. Late September and early October find you enjoying friendships and travel. During the last half of October Mars will square Saturn bringing the 8th house into play. Be careful of investments and other projects suggested by an adventurous type. Near the Full Moon eclipse on October 27 there can be a message from the spirit realm with important guidance regarding daily work and health care. Resist the temptation to be overly critical during the days preceding All Hallows. Tolerance and appreciation on your part will open more doors.

November marks the beginning of a long Mercury passage conjunct your Sun and Pluto in Sagittarius. This will continue through the early days of 2005. Holiday travel can be very memorable. A chance to correct ongoing problems will present itself. Gather information and sharpen skills. The Sagittarius New Moon on December 11 illuminates this pattern's focus. Venus enters your sign shortly before Yule. Your charm and appeal are in top form during the holidays. A special birthday or New Year's invitation brings happiness. Finances will be beneficially affected too. A long anticipated purchase provides great enjoyment. The good times roll on until January 9. Throughout the rest of January through February 5 the presence of a Mars passage through your sign will generate a more hectic pace. Control anger and impatience. You'll be motivated and can accomplish much, but don't push too hard or overreact. Light a pale blue candle at Candlemas and dedicate it to a visualization of peace.

During February Neptune will tinge Mercury and Venus in the 3rd house. Trust your instincts about a new neighbor. Work to communicate with a brother or sister. Nuances and subtleties abound. In early March planets will gather in your home and family sector. Welcome a new relative or visitor into the household by generating a sense of a safe haven. A residential move or home improvement would be successful. The New Moon on March 10 will be near Uranus and can reveal the scope of domestic changes. A Mercury–Mars square in cardinal signs can make March a rather expensive month regarding love and leisure time activities. Don't argue about finances with a child or other loved one. Seek creative ways to enjoy free hours without jeopardizing your security. As winter ends, resolve to enjoy all that you already have.

HEALTH

Recognizing and controlling temptation is important now. Pluto's influence in your birth sign can lead you into stressful activities or create a tendency to overindulge. With sensual Taurus ruling your health sector it's easy to binge on rich or exotic dishes near the time of the October 27 Taurus eclipse. Focus on a healthy lifestyle throughout the autumn months. Address health concerns in May and October.

LOVE

Venus will make a long passage through your 7th house of marriage this year. Between early April and Lammastide you'll be the object of admiration and loyal devotion. An existing relationship can strengthen or a new one develop. The potentials for this happy trend are best during late July when a proposal could be issued or accepted. A talented and well mannered person includes you in plans and invitations. Social prospects near your birthday should be happy as well.

Pets are often the first love of Sagittarians. Make certain that a romantic interest will be good to your animal companions.

SPIRITUALITY

With mystical Neptune in your 3rd house all year, keeping a journal can be very worthwhile in your quest for spiritual growth. Record Tarot spreads and note omens. During July a Mars transit shows that practicing yoga or martial arts would awaken a new spiritual understanding. A lively discussion revolving around spiritual growth can ensue near Lammas. Mythology can be especially helpful to you this year. Review the archetypal messages encoded in the ancient tales of the classical gods and goddesses to facilitate spiritual awareness.

FINANCE

The year will begin with Jupiter forming a square to both Uranus and Pluto in mutable signs. In some respect this can be a gambler's aspect. Keep credit cards in check and exercise great care in speculation. Saturn will transit your 8th house. Plan carefully for payment of taxes, insurance policies, and in meeting financial obligations to your others. The settling of an estate could impact your security. Seek ways to make the most of any hidden assets. After the autumn equinox Jupiter will change signs and better financial situations will develop.

CAPRICORN

The year ahead for those
born under the sign of the Goat
December 22–January 20

Capricorn's focus revolves around concepts of shifting values. This birth sign finds the individual seeking identification with a larger collectivity. Personal achievement leads to the establishment of new civilization while turning away from shallowness. Penetrating yet cautious, a flair for business and a yearning for practical achievement motivate you. In classical myth Pan, the goat god, charms and promises joy to those who listen to his music. For his bravery during the battle with the Titans, Pan was rewarded with a fish tail, a symbol of the goat's duality and versatility.

The urge to get started on important work burns within you as the spring begins. The Aries Sun squares Saturn, your ruler, until the end of March. You feel pressure to take action. Until April 3 Venus spreads delight in your love sector. Health will be a focus throughout most of April, for Gemini transits will be highlighting your 6th house. At the same time Mercury, ruler of the 6th, will be retrograde. Be aware of what your health history indicates. Work at fitness. You will be uncertain of what you really want as the lunar eclipse of May 4 approaches. This will affect your 11th house and links to long-term wishes and plans. Overcome confusion by spending the Beltane sabbat in divination.

On May 16 Mercury joins the Sun in Taurus to brighten your love and pleasure sector. There may be a couple of admirers from which to choose. During June, Mars and Saturn march together through your opposing sign of Cancer. The 7th and 1st houses are involved. A confrontation might be brewing; seek legal counsel if need be. Pull away from associates who demand too much. This is not the time for marriage or other commitments. The Full Moon on July 2 in your sign heightens your intuition. Gather information and make decisions near then.

Jupiter is powerfully aspected in Virgo during July and August. This forms a graceful trine to your Sun from the 9th house. A plan for growth develops. Keep your faith strong, but act independently. Just before Lammastide Mercury will also enter Virgo. A favorable cycle for study and journeys commences. Prepare travel amulets at the sabbat on August 1.

On August 7 Venus enters your partnership sector. In both love and business people become more giving and thoughtful. Mars' passage into Virgo on August 10 finds your physical vitality improving. Depression lifts, and your faith helps you to carry plans forward. The autumn equinox finds a three planet stellium in your 9th house. Focus on performing a formal ritual to honor the new season. The favorable presence of planetary transits in Virgo, bearer of the sheaf, reveals that whole grain dishes will have special healing qualities for you now.

Throughout October Mars will move through your 10th house while squaring both Saturn and your Sun. There's a new urge to contribute on a professional level. Take time to relax, and keep anger in check. Through discipline and organization you will advance. Venus will enter Virgo on October 3. From then until just before All Hallows admiration and love come your way. You'll find added happiness in cultural interests. From mid-October through November 3 a positive Mercury aspect involving your 11th house brings helpful guidance from friends. It's a good time to seek an opinion or request advice. A conversation on Halloween can be very significant.

Saturn begins a long retrograde cycle in November. There will be opportunities to reconnect with old associates as the late autumn days shorten. Purchase an attractive sundial, clock, or hourglass and say a blessing over it. This will act as a charm to help you manage time well. You'll feel grateful, as there are many near you who have so much less to work with. A strong 12th house during December may find you feeling introspective. Make the most of quiet, private time. At Yuletide there will be more ease of expression. Don't let an old regret cloud your happiness–this is futile. Instead offset vague guilt by performing good actions in the here and now.

By January 10 both Mercury and Venus begin transits in your birth sign. At Candlemas you can solve problems, arrange ventures, and make valuable social contacts. It's a wonderful time to select artwork or to shop for clothes. As February commences the Sun will join Neptune in Aquarius, activating your 2nd house of money. Finance is always one of your favorite topics, but this is especially true through Valentine's Day. There can be some confusion concerning exactly what your monetary circumstances are. First impressions should be heeded as you make financial plans now. On February 6 vigorous Mars enters your sign where it will remain through the end of the winter, empowering you. Direct your energies fairly and compassionately in all dealings. Much is completed, but don't push yourself or others too hard.

On March 4 Mercury enters Aries, completing a grand cross in cardinal signs. Since all four of the angles in your chart will be involved in this dynamic pattern many projects are unfolding simultaneously. Humor and patience will help. List priorities and stick to a reasonable schedule if you feel temporarily overwhelmed.

HEALTH

Venus will remain in your health sector from early April until early August. The healing power of touch can be experienced under this trend. This links to receiving love from others and feeling its healing force, or by becoming involved in interests which you enjoy. Either way, surrounding yourself with loving energies will be beneficial. Since Venus is in Gemini, the zodiacal communicator, reading and talking about your health situations will also help.

LOVE

Loved ones need your understanding and support now, for Saturn will be in your 7th house of relationships all year. Be realistic about your expectations. A long-term partnership might run its course. If this is true, a healing comes through release. A loved one can show vulnerability. Your support and understanding mean a great deal to one who cares for you. The April 19 eclipse will impact family life. A relative makes a surprise announcement near that time. The October 27 Taurus eclipse falls directly in your 5th house. Love will have sparkle and bring some surprises by the year's end.

SPIRITUALITY

Spring through the autumn equinox marks a very favorable time to make spiritual pilgrimages. Jupiter in Virgo will highlight your 9th house. Visiting pyramids, sacred mountains, and legendary ruins will inspire and uplift you. If that's not possible, watch films. Then read about the history of the craft in order to develop a deeper understanding of mystical doctrines. Prepare a presentation about spells and folk charms from another country to offer your coven or study group. As you share this knowledge, you will delight the old gods while enhancing your own insight.

FINANCE

Your career situation is changing. Adapt to current worldwide economic trends and progressive developments in your field. Autumn will be significant, for it brings both the October 13 eclipse in your 10th house and the onset of a year-long Jupiter transit in the same sector. Libra rules your 10th house of achievement and fortune. This sign is all about interaction with others. Remember the value of networking and improving your people skills. Maintain a balance between personal and professional life. Being well-rounded will better prepare you to reach your goals.

AQUARIUS

*The year ahead for those
born under the sign of the Water Bearer*
January 21–February 19

Symbolized by the human figure pouring generously, Aquarius is concerned with large issues. The direction society is taking and advocating needed changes are important. A pure impulse of dynamic creation is present with this birth sign. This inventive and unpredictable individualist shows a fixed stubborn side. Ganymede, cup bearer to Jupiter, is identified with the sign of Aquarius.

With the vernal equinox Venus is placed in your 4th house, favoring home life. Honor the day with a gathering at your dwelling. Share memories of long cherished traditions linked to your heritage. Early April marks the start of a long Venus trine aspect in your romance sector. Since Gemini, your brother air sign, is involved true happiness in a really good relationship can be attained by Lammastide. However, while Venus is retrograde from mid-May through June, be especially patient and very sincere. There can be an old hurdle to surmount before love is free to grow. It will.

The first half of May favors travel. Mercury will wing rapidly through the 3rd house making a sextile to your Sun. Accept an invitation for Beltane. Health care is likely to be important from late May through Midsummer Eve. Mars will stir in the 6th house and form a quincunx aspect. Seek ways to release stress. Make certain foods and beverages are fresh, and use sun protection when outside. During July compromise is important. Both Mars and Mercury

will oppose you. Remember, there are at least two sides to every story. Rigidity can impede progress. The Full Moon of July 31 is a rare and magical Blue Moon. It falls in your birth sign and promises that Lammas will be very special this year. You'll be appreciated, and an important point is made or a goal reached. Since there is a conjunction with Neptune to this lunation, focus on angel magic. An image of an angel on your altar will act as a catalyst for contact with celestial beings now.

August brings an emphasis on Virgo planets in your 8th house. Income can be enhanced by a tax refund, insurance settlement, or a return on an investment. Others tend to be generous if you seek financial advice or assistance. This sector also has a link with the afterlife. A message from a loved one who has passed on may comfort you. September 7 finds Venus entering your 7th house of relationships. A phase begins when you'll be sought after as a partner, both businesswise and personally. Your sensitivity and thoughtfulness win the loyalty of another by the autumn equinox. At the end of September Jupiter begins a year-long passage through Libra. It trines Neptune in your birth sign and involves the 9th house. Spiritual growth assumes greater importance. Old limitations dissolve. For those involved in educational programs the rewards will be especially great. Relationships between grandparents and grandchildren are mutually enjoyable in the weeks ahead.

The last half of October brings an urge to communicate with loved ones about career matters. Mercury creates a tense aspect in your 10th house. The eclipse on October 27 brings some complications related to home and family situations. Gather information; make sure there is a meeting of the minds. You might find yourself working in a different place with some new people. A move may be considered. A favorable Mars aspect gives you plenty of energy to handle this with aplomb by All Hallows' Eve. During the first three weeks of November Venus trines your Sun. Travel sets the scene for a joyful love experience. Mystical poetry, art, and other expressions of beauty can heighten spirituality in the weeks before Thanksgiving. Your ruler, Uranus, completes a long retrograde during November. As Yule nears it's easier to move forward. Old disappointments fade in significance. Pluto and other Sagittarius transits highlight your 11th house during November and December. New acquaintances are about to enliven your social circle, but use discretion if someone seems a little too complex or controversial.

During January several transits in your 12th house will open you to a deeper appreciation of nature and wildlife. Observe wild birds, raccoons or other creatures. A ritual to protect and commune with them at the New Moon on January 10 can be very effective. Near Candlemas Mercury, Venus, and Neptune all begin to cluster in conjunction with your Sun. February ushers in a time of visions, ideas and creativity. You're charming and charismatic. Finances are a focus after February 16. Mercury, the Sun, Uranus, and Venus are all moving through or toward your 2nd house of security by the month's end. The sense of well-being that enough cash flow assures is appreciated now.

Seek to release any hidden anger about the financial decisions of another during March. Mars in Capricorn will be opposing retrograde Saturn. This can bring some temporary frustration with how associates perform job duties and handle their assets. From the 5th on Mercury will be in Aries, making everyone a bit outspoken. Reread letters before sending them, and keep your tone pleasant in conversation. Consider carefully before letting an argument ensue.

HEALTH
Saturn in Cancer highlights your health sector this year. Be patient with your body. Allow treatments and health care programs enough time to work. Time-honored home remedies can treat minor ailments successfully. Your circulatory system and glands are always vulnerable. Massage can be helpful. Take steps to maintain comfort amid temperature extremes too. This can be as simple as just keeping a shawl handy when the wind brings a chill.

LOVE
The spring and summer are most promising for love as Venus brightens your 5th house of romance from April until August. Since airy Gemini rules your affections, seek a partner who is well spoken, attractive and mentally stimulating. A degree of freedom when in a committed situation is essential to your happiness. Make certain that you enjoy the company of the friends of a companion who is winning your heart. Then make certain your prospective partner's feelings are mutual concerning your friends. Keep in mind that you may especially enjoy exchanging notes with a new prospect who has suddenly caught your eye.

SPIRITUALITY
On September 24 Jupiter will begin a year-long passage through Libra. This involves your area of faith and spiritual awakening. The autumn and winter months will find your spiritual expression taking a new direction. You could ask friends about their beliefs and you might enjoy honoring their holy days with them. Why not visit an unfamiliar place of worship and observe how a service or ceremony impacts you? There is a subtle link with the Far East. Mystical traditions from Tibet, China, and Japan can provide a meaningful and interesting focus.

FINANCE
Uranus will create some chaos in your financial sector the year long. However, it is in a mutual reception with Neptune in Aquarius and flowing in a trine with Saturn in Cancer. This assures that it will be possible to escape any serious financial difficulties with relative ease. There can be some unexpected opportunities to add to your income. Perfect a new, salable job skill. With Saturn's influence present, take care to keep working circumstances comfortable and compatible. Maintain patience about financial matters. Gradual, steady effort on your part brings rewards. Speculation is more favorably undertaken from October on than it would have been earlier in the year.

PISCES

*The year ahead for those
born under the sign of the Fish*
February 20–March 20

Pisces has a unique position amongst the twelve zodiac signs. It marks both the end of the old year and the start of a new cycle. The Fish swim backward and forward, anticipating a new growth cycle while savoring and accepting the old. Dreamy Pisces is linked to compassion, sacrifice, and illusions. There is an introspective kindness present. Venus and Cupid leapt into the river Euphrates to escape pursuit. Two noble fish saved them from drowning. The Pisces were rewarded with a place in the heavens.

Spring cleaning has a literal meaning for you this year. With the coming of the new season, Mars is in Gemini at a square to your Sun. This creates a stir in your home and family sector. Seek ways to make your residence more comfortable. A family member can be a trifle volatile. On April 3 Venus joins Mars and happier times begin. After Beltane Venus' influence reigns supreme in your 4th house of residence. Between May and August great blessings will come to hearth and home.

On May 17 Neptune, your ruler, and Venus turn retrograde. Questions of sincerity arise. The 12th house is involved. Dreams are highly symbolic and must be interpreted carefully. The first three weeks of June bring ample opportunities for recreation and love, as your 5th house is accented. June 21–July 4 Mercury will move rapidly through Cancer, supported by the solar transit. It's a wonderful time for learn-ing and problem-solving, as intellectual capacity is in peak form. Take note of ideas that occur now, they can prove useful later.

Use the last three weeks of July to make progress with health and fitness regimes as Leo transits accent your 6th house of wellness. At Lammastide Virgo planets Jupiter, Mercury, and, from August 10 on, Mars will form an opposition to your Sun from the 7th house. Others take action involving you. A partnership is forming which could be a very important part of your future. Venus hovers in your romance sector while moving through Cancer, your sister water sign. This is marvelous for love prospects from August 7–September 5. The Full Moon on August 29 conjoins Uranus in your sign. A wonderful four-week cycle begins for the study of astrology and alternative thought. You'll gain a deeper awareness of who you are and what your life means by the autumn equinox.

At the end of September your 8th house will be activated by Mars, Jupiter, and the Sun. All are in Libra. Prepare for a few secrets to come to light. Explore investments and other strategies to establish long-term financial security. Throughout most of October charming Venus moves quickly through your 7th house, bringing well mannered and talented people to you. It's also a favorable trend for settling any legal matters or other disputes amicably. The solar eclipse on October 13 brings a glimpse into the motivations of others as well as a message from the spirit world. From October 15 through Samhain Mercury in Scorpio creates a good aspect pattern in your 9th house. Seize an opportunity to travel, especially if you can visit with and learn from other witches in the process. This is an optimum time to prepare some writing for publication.

During November, first Pluto and Mercury and then the Sun highlight your 10th house. You'll be more visible in your professional sphere and could acquire a bit of notoriety. There's a competitive quality present. On November 8 Saturn turns retrograde in Cancer in your 5th house. Relationships with children follow old patterns. Romance has a stable and comforting quality. Return to a creative project or hobby that was abandoned previously. As Thanksgiving nears Venus smiles at you with a transit through Scorpio. A friend from another ethnic or spiritual background proves to be good company. Romantic prospects and seasonal travel trends are excellent. December opens with an upbeat Mars aspect to your Sun, giving you a vigorous sparkle through the 24th. You'll feel like initiating celebrations and other projects. The last week of December finds five planets in mutable signs. This will be hectic. Get organized in preparation for 2005. Take time to release stress by dancing to a favorite tune or burning an aromatic candle.

January begins with Mercury close to a conjunction with Pluto near your midheaven. Questions of status and credibility could arise. Don't be impatient or argumentative. The New Moon on January 10 brings helpful group support. It marks the start of a sextile in your 11th house from Capricorn transits. Late January is wonderful for forming goals and determining what you desire most. Crystal gazing or dowsing with a pendulum bring insights. A renewed stability comforts you as Candlemas approaches.

February finds Aquarius transits joining Neptune in your 12th house, activating your inner life and your dreams. Time spent alone will be treasured. A creative project could begin to take form while you're enjoying a solitary walk. On February 17 Mercury enters your sign where it will conjoin Uranus. The remainder of the month is wonderful for the study of metaphysics, including astrology. Extra travel is likely near your birthday. A telephone call or other message is especially meaningful. March brings great happiness. Venus will dance through Pisces hand in hand with Uranus. You'll enjoy purchasing items you've longed to acquire. Love, appreciation, and compliments surround you as the year concludes.

HEALTH
Neptune opposes your 6th house of health all year, accenting the importance of being in tune with yourself. Analyze which foods, lifestyle factors, and exercise programs are apropos. The Neptune opposition emphasizes that associates can impact your wellbeing. Avoid those who might be unwell or who merely upset you. Be sure to get a second opinion concerning diagnosis and health care options. All might not be as it seems initially.

LOVE
Serious Saturn in Cancer makes a trine in your love sector the year long. A relationship becomes more stable. The company of someone a generation older or younger can grow into a romantic involvement. Working on worthwhile projects together would facilitate true and lasting love now. You could even successfully juggle a romantic situation with a coworker. A new maturity beneficially impacts your approach to love affairs. You grow weary of those who play games. Mutual accomplishment will have more appeal. August and early September finds Venus conjunct Saturn. This ushers in an especially comforting, calming type of love situation.

SPIRITUALITY
The May 4 eclipse at the Full Moon just after May Day strongly activates your 9th house. This promises a heightened awareness of the deeper meaning of life. It sets the pace for spiritual growth during the rest of the year. Since the eclipse is in Scorpio, refining and purifying desires, past life studies, and forgiveness will play a role in awakening higher thought.

FINANCE
Patience is a virtue when planning finances this year. Fiery Mars and Aries rule your 2nd house, the indicator of monetary matters. Use care in investigating the practicality of new schemes. The April 19 eclipse in Aries promises some changes in the source of income or salable job skills. Be receptive to growth and all will be well. Others will make suggestions regarding finance through the autumn equinox, for Jupiter will be in opposition until then. A business partnership at this time could be worth considering.

THE SORCERER'S CAVE

There is evidence that ritual practices were performed in caves and some of them appear to have been holy places. The most notable example is the cave of the Trois Frères at Ariège in France, where a strange half-human, half-animal figure dominates an inner cavern.

— MAN, MYTH & MAGIC

Ordeal and enlightenment define the process of initiation. Herbert Kühn describes his visit to the cavern of the sorcerer in just such terms.

"The tunnel is not much broader than my shoulders, nor higher. I can hear the others before me groaning and see how slowly their lamps push on. With our arms pressed close to our sides, we wriggle forward on our stomachs, like snakes. The passage, in places, is hardly a foot high, so that you have to lay your face right on the earth...you cannot lift your head; you cannot breathe. And so, yard by yard, one struggles on. Nobody talks. It is terrible to have the roof so close to one's head. And the roof is very hard: I bump it, time and again. Will this thing never end? Then, suddenly, we are through, and everybody breathes. It is like a redemption.

"The hall in which we are now standing is gigantic. We let the lights of the lamps run along the ceiling and walls; a majestic room—and there, finally, are the pictures. From top to bottom a whole wall is covered with engravings. The surface has been worked with tools of stone, and there we see marshaled the beasts that lived at that time in southern France: the mammoth, rhinoceros, bison, wild horse, bear, wild ass, reindeer, wolverine, musk ox; also the smaller animals appear: snowy owls, hares, and fish.

"The style is everywhere firm and full of life, not in paint, but engraved, fixing forever the momentary turns, leaps, and flashes of the animal kingdom in a teeming tumult of everlasting life. And above them all, predominant—at the opposite end of the sanctuary to the hole through which we have emerged, some fifteen feet above the level of the floor, in a craggy apse — watching, staring at our arrival with unflinching eyes, is the now famous Sorcerer of Les Trois Frères, presiding over the animals there assembled. He is poised in profile in a dancing posture, but the antlered head is turned to face the hall. It is the only picture in the whole gallery rendered in black paint. An eerie, thrilling sight."

The cave called *Les Trois Frères* (The Three Brothers) is named for the three sons of the Count Bégouën, who, with their father, discovered and explored the vast cavern shortly before the outbreak of World War I. The art belongs to the last milennia of the Paleolithic Age, c. 14,000 B. C.

Tracings of cave art made by Abbé Henri Breuil

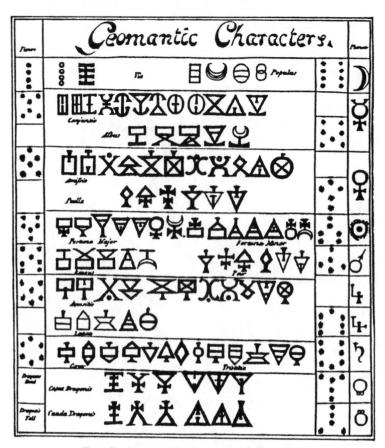

From *The Magus* by Francis Barrett, London, 1801

EARTH PROPHECY

Geomancy, from the Greek words *geo*, the earth and *manteia,* prophecy, originated centuries ago in the Arab world where the art of sand-divining is still in common practice. Renowned author and magician Cornelius Agrippa introduced geomantic principles to literate Europeans in his *Occult Philosophy*, Volume II, published in Antwerp in 1531. "The Art of the Little Dots," as geomancy was called in 17th-century France, enjoyed a vogue at the court of Louis XIV, where it was regarded as a most reliable oracle. Its answers, then and now, prove provocative, surprising, and more often than not, right on the mark.

The curious fact about geomancy is that it doesn't require sand or earth to be effective. The primary aim is to create a vertical pattern of four rows composed of single and double dots. One dot stands for an odd number.

Two dots represent an even number. Classically, the querent makes a random series of holes in the earth with a polished stick. The seer then isolates a certain group and interprets its significance. Another simple and direct method requires only thought, pen, and paper:

Decide on four single digit numbers. You might roll dice, draw playing cards, or just call four to mind as you would for a lottery. Observe one strict rule: concentrate intently on your question while the decision is made. Suppose the numbers you choose are four, two, five, seven.

4 - even.   • •
2 - even.   • •
5 - odd.   •
7 - odd.   •

Match the pattern to one of the 16 possible combinations and you will find it means *Fortuna Major*, a good-luck portent.

Via, the way. Cultivate patience, for life itself moves slowly in a wandering manner. Bright hope beckons from afar. Expect some detours. Element: Water. Planet: Moon. Sign: Cancer.

Populus, reunion with humanity. Understand the crowd, but bend not to popular opinion. Be practical and maintain quiet confidence. Avoid disorder. Element: Water. Planet: Moon. Sign: Cancer.

Conjunctio, meeting. Rely on integrated and coordinated effort. Don't lose sight of the primary goal. Proceed in harmony. Communicate to reach concord. Element: Earth. Planet: Mercury. Sign: Virgo.

Albus, white, spirituality. Purity of heart and serenity of spirit are your gifts. Protect your home from negative forces. Seek to find a clear horizon. Element: Air. Planet: Mercury. Sign: Gemini.

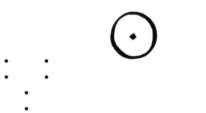

Amissio, loss. Failure and diminution result from passivity. The path of least resistance has many dangers. Take heart and renew your courage. Element: Air. Planet: Venus. Sign: Libra.

Puella, femininity, softness. Look for gentleness. Your answer will come in solitude. Escape stress to find true value. Element: Earth. Planet: Venus. Sign: Taurus.

Fortuna major, splendor, good fortune. You've won a victory with honor. Now you must learn to build upon it. Move on. Element: Fire. Planet: Sun. Sign: Leo.

Fortuna minor, success. Worldly success is welcome, not outstanding and not always moral. A time to explore deeper levels of being. Element: Fire. Planet: Sun. Sign: Leo.

Rubeus, red, earthiness. Passion overrides good sense. Withdraw until the smoke from the battle clears away. Element: Fire. Planet: Mars. Sign: Aries.

Puer, masculinity and solidity. Forthright action is indicated. Take the direct path, but shun violence. Avoid deceit. Element: Fire. Planet: Mars. Sign: Scorpio.

Acquisitio, gain. Growth is indicated. Both material and moral success. Beware of taking advantage of those less fortunate. To cheat is to lose. Element: Air. Planet: Jupiter. Sign: Pisces.

Laetitia, happiness, joy. A cycle is completed. Wisdom is gained. An end is a beginning. Give praise to those who nurture thee. Element: Air. Planet: Jupiter. Sign: Sagittarius.

Carcer, prison, isolation. Free yourself from that which restrains and hinders individual progress. Break the chains of habit. Element: Earth. Planet: Saturn. Sign: Capricorn.

Tristitia, misfortune. Restriction and anxiety cloud the question. Review the alternatives. Refuse to accept despair on any terms. Element: Earth. Planet: Saturn. Sign: Aquarius.

Caput draconis, head of the dragon. Peace, inner happiness, fruitfulness will be yours. All pleasures are the products of natural forces. Element: Air. Planet: Moon in ascending node. Sign: Virgo.

Cauda draconis, dragon tail. Outer happiness is threatened by pernicious and destructive forces. Beware of discord. Be alert to possible betrayal. Element: Earth. Planet: Moon in descending node. Sign: Libra.

SACRED SERPENT MOUND

Whether snake images make one recoil in horror or feel charmed and awed, seldom does the topic meet with indifference. Since prehistoric times few creatures command the same sense of mystery, emotion and genuine fascination. In southern Ohio, a group of Native Americans honored the snake by building a gigantic serpent replica of stone and earth. The fabulous creature stretches 1,348 feet, the body is about 20 feet wide and varies in height from two to six feet. Dubbed Serpent Mound, this intriguing creation appears to perpetually uncoil its body over more than a quarter of a mile along a remote and wild ridge. The indigenous culture which created Serpent Mound left no written history. Archaeologists don't know whether the sculpture was intended as a gesture of veneration or repulsion.

Since at least 1848, visitors have enjoyed visiting and speculating about the form. In 1883 Frederic Ward Putnam, a scientist with vision, realized that Serpent Mound was being destroyed by vandalism and erosion. He raised funds through Harvard University to purchase the mound for a public park. A 25-foot observation tower was erected by the Ohio Historical Society 25 years later, providing visitors with a view of the whole serpent. A museum offers information about the history of the site. Photos of picnics enjoyed by visitors over a hundred years ago are displayed with pottery and other artifacts, including tiny ceramic replicas of snakes uncovered during excavation.

Serpent Mound lies along the northern portion of the Ohio bluegrass region. It was never covered by glaciers and has flora and fauna more similar to that of Kentucky than the rest of the Midwest. Red cedar thickets, Ohio buckeye, maple, American beech and a variety of wildflowers make the surrounding countryside a rich and lovely place to explore. Between the vernal equinox and May Day the area is especially wonderful. Visitors can expect early spring to bring a special treat; the lawns surrounding Serpent Mound itself are carpeted with blue violets.

Looking at this splendid monument, tourists wonder why the big snake was built and by whom. There are no human remains present to indicate a burial mound. In 1991 a group of archaeologists used the most sophisticated techniques to probe the mystery. Radiocarbon dating of small pieces of charcoal found in an undisturbed part of the mound yielded the date 1070 A.D., nearly a thousand years ago. They concluded that it was built by the Fort Ancient peoples, a culture which followed the Adena and Hopewell Mound Builders. There is a similarity to divine feathered serpents, Quetzalcoatl of the Aztecs and Kukulcan of the Mayas. Traditions from the Algonquian tribe of Lake Superior tell of a lake serpent that provided copper from its horns, while the Delaware Indians of Ohio feared an evil river snake. The Wyandot Indians have the same word for "snake" as they do for mysterious evil power. But the Shawnees, another Ohio tribe, use the term *manito* to describe both snakes and spiritual awareness. This reflects the concept of kundalini as the powerful healing snake force within as identified by contemporary mystics and yoga practitioners.

About 1900 a Reverend Landon West saw the effigy as representative of the biblical snake from the Garden of Eden. The small mound or tongue in the front of the head he felt showed how its jaws grasped an apple-shaped fruit to symbolize the choice between good and evil. Other visitors recalled the fiery visit of Halley's Comet in 1066. This appearance of Halley's comet almost exactly coincides with the radiocarbon dating of the mound's construction. Perhaps the cosmic spectacle was seen as a gleaming sky serpent that the Amerindians felt should be honored.

Before damage was done, early drawings of the Serpent Mound showed smaller projections around the serpent's head. These could have been a series of feathers, a protruding forked tongue,

GREAT SERPENT MOUND
Detail from a diagram made
by Squire and Davis, 1846

or frogs about to be swallowed. Perhaps this was a clue that the serpent was one that might have swallowed the Sun and Moon during eclipses, an early common metaphor.

During the 1980's and 1990's several prominent astronomers examined Serpent Mound for astronomical alignments. Two of them, Robert Fletcher and Terry Cameron, demonstrated that a line drawn along the upper body of the structure across the center oval aligns with the setting Sun in the summer solstice. They continued to map the peaks of the three undulating humps from head to tail to find alignments with the sunrises at the summer solstice, autumn and spring equinoxes and the winter solstice. This suggests that the snake was used as an astrology calendar for ritual worship and to time planting and harvest cycles.

The deep sense of beauty and mystery surrounding the structure is well worth experiencing. Part of the appeal lies in the knowledge that we will never really know exactly why it was built or by whom. The site has even provided the inspiration for a recording of Native American themed music called *Serpent Mound*. Many sensitives believe that this superb structure is an important power vortex, a sacred site of great significance.

The Serpent Mound Park is located on State Road 73, 4 miles northwest of Locust Grove, Ohio. Visitors arriving from Cincinnati travel east on Highway 50. The Serpent Mound Memorial Park museum and gift shop are open daily. There is a small admission charge.

— DIKKI-JO MULLEN

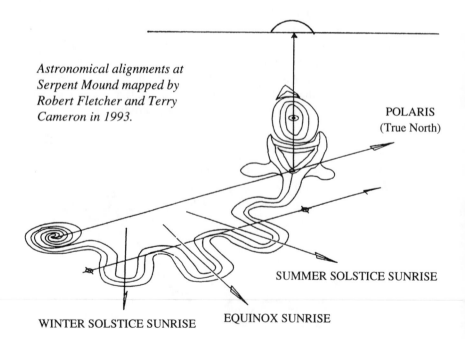

Astronomical alignments at Serpent Mound mapped by Robert Fletcher and Terry Cameron in 1993.

POLARIS
(True North)

SUMMER SOLSTICE SUNRISE

WINTER SOLSTICE SUNRISE

EQUINOX SUNRISE

Herbs of Witchery

Certain herbs acquire greater power under stress and seem to thrive in the garden no one tends — the wild. Those listed below are all alien plants, garden escapes, here now masquerading as wildflowers or weeds. These ancient specimens perennially grace roadsides, railroad tracks, old meadows, vacant lots, swamps, woods, pine barrens and other waste places. You need only collect the smallest bouquets from most and a dozen or so leaves from the larger variety of herbs. Pleasant and rewarding, the quest is known from olden days as "wildcrafting."

Broom (*Cytisus scoparius*): A sprig of its yellow flowers in a soldier's cap lent courage in battle. The herb blooms in sandy soil from May through June. Wave a stalk in the air to raise a wind.

Clover (*Trifolium pratense*): Magic often favors a humble site and common clover is a case in point. Its three-leaf form is linked with the goddess Hecate. Called "trefoil" in old herbals that recommend its use in love charms. The plant blooms red-purple from May to September.

Fumitory (*Fumaria officinalis*): The gray-green foliage looks like smoke rising from the earth, and smoke from burning dried and crumbled fumitory herb purifies an atmosphere for magical work. Rose flowers with purple tips bloom from May to August.

Mullein (*Verbascum thapsus*): From June to September many roadsides are brightened by the presence of the large yellow-flowered plant once called "The Hag's Taper." Collect its flannel-textured leaves to dry and beat to a powder. Use as a substitute for "graveyard dust," often required for certain spells.

Orpine (*Sedum telephium*): Orpine's folk name is "Midsummer Men." A maiden with romance on her mind was advised to collect a single pink blossom of orpine in silence and sleep with it beneath her pillow in order to dream of the man who would someday win her heart. The herb can be found during August and September in once-cultivated fields or along roadways.

St. John's wort (*Hypericum perforatum*): This sacred herb adorned with yellow flowers blooms from June to

September. Its primary use in witchcraft is to strengthen willpower and protect its bearer from harm.

Tansy (*Tanacetum vulgare*): Its stalks are topped with bright golden buttons and its fernlike leaves emit a strong pleasant smell. The dried flowerheads and seeds wrapped in tissue paper guard treasured possessions. Tansy blooms from July to September.

Vervain (*Verbena officinalis*): The plant held sacred by the most diverse European cultures is quite modest to the eye. Its spikes of tiny lilac flowers with five petals comes to bloom from June to October.

Yarrow (*Achillea millefolium*): Yarrow is in evidence from June to August. A tight cluster of tiny dull white petals forms the flat flowerhead. Its aromatic leaves are fernlike. Yarrow is primarily a divinatory herb and often added to incense for that purpose. The dried, powdered flowers and leaves of the plant are part of many love charms.

in the garden

Some herbal perennials prefer the shelter of a garden and yield best when tended with loving care. A witch plants leafy, above-ground crops while the moon is waxing to full. Seed sown from full to last quarter especially benefit perennials. The moon's place should be in one of the water signs — Cancer, Scorpio, Pisces. A moon in Libra is believed to favor flowering

herbs. All the plants listed range between two to three feet tall with the exception of periwinkle, a creeping ground cover.

Hyssop (*Hyssopus officinalis*): Dark green leaves and blue, pink or white flowers add color to the herb garden. This highly aromatic herb is used in magic for purification and protection. It is easily grown from seed.

Lavender (*Lavendula officinalis*): This is one of the nine herbs cast into the sacred fires of summer solstice eve. Its primary quality is fragrance and spikes of pale purple flowers are carried to attract the opposite sex.

Monkshood (*Aconitum napellus*): A deadly poison plant to be sure, but its beauty is beyond compare. Blue-purple flowers bloom from late summer to frost. Monkshood prefers shade and well-drained soil.

Mugwort (*Artemisia vulgaris*): Because of its invasive nature, some say mugwort deserves no place in the herb garden. But it may be wise to plant one clump by itself, for this is an herb with a myriad of mystic virtues. The dried leaves fill dream pillows. Carry a sprig on a journey to prevent fatigue. A wreath over the doorway protects the home from intruders.

Periwinkle (*Vinca minor*): This magic plant of shiny evergreen leaves and delicate pinwheels of lavender-blue flowers deserves its mystic reputation. Not only does it repel evil, it revives fading love and channels wayward thought.

Sage (*Salvia officinalis*): Burn dried sage leaves in the home to erase any lingering negativity after the departure of an unpleasant visitor or the receipt of a disappointing phone call. One of the most useful and satisfying garden plants, sage is strong and hardy. Cooks rely on its flavor.

Southernwood (*Artemisia abrotanum*): A unique herb that may become your favorite, for it offers a haunting scent and quiet shrublike beauty. While it receives little attention in old herbals or books about magic, southernwood blends well with many incenses, adding a curious element of surprise.

Tarragon (*Artemisia dracunculus*): The Latin name means "little dragon of Artemis," and the herb is believed to instill its wearer with the bravery attributed to the goddess of the hunt. Carry a sprig when you anticipate trouble. A handsome plant and a noble addition to any garden, tarragon is a treasure in the culinary art.

Wormwood (*Artemisia absinthium*): A proud plant of silvery leaves, wormwood contributes distinction to an herb garden. Associated with Mars and warriors as well as the Greek goddess of the hunt, wormwood guards against evil spirits. Combine its dried leaves with incense to aid and abet clairvoyance.

for the home

The indoor garden of a witch follows an old rule of keeping color, fragrance and magic alive during the dark season of winter. Along with bright geraniums for color, you may add the scent and magic of sacred herbs, for several will flourish as house plants.

Aloe (*Aloe vera*): A practical witch keeps an aloe plant close at hand in case of burns. Slit a frond to release the juice that immediately provides comfort and healing.

Catnip (*Nepeta cataria*): The herb is mainly grown for the pleasure it brings to cats. Long ago the minty plant acquired a reputation as a fertility charm. A tea made from its dried leaves restores confidence.

Germander (*Teucrium chamaedrys*): A lovely pine scent and the beauty of its dark green, glossy leaves and pale pink flowers recommend germander as an attractive pot plant. The French call it "little oak," for its form and leaves resemble that noble tree.

From *Witches All*, a treasury from past editions of *The Witches' Almanac*.

Jasmine (*Jasminum officinale*): This night-blooming plant has a natural association with love, for its scent is hauntingly lovely befitting that tender emotion. Scores of love charms employ the dried blossoms of jasmine, which look like tiny white trumpets ending in a star.

Laurel (*Laurus nobilis*): Bay or sweet laurel is more a tree than an herb. As a tub plant, laurel may reach a height of four to six feet. Its old leaves fall only when new ones develop, so the tree is always green, a true emblem of immortality.

Myrtle (M*yrtus communis*): Herbal lore suggests myrtle is an emblem of love, fertility and marriage. A tub plant with a profusion of delicate bright green leaves and tiny white puff blossoms, a myrtle will grace any solarium. A myrtle bough symbolizes all new beginnings.

Rosemary (*Rosmarinus officinalis*): An essential herb in the indoor garden, with a great variety of magical virtues. The Latin name translates as "dew of the sea," and its gray-green needles of foliage and exquisite blue-lavender flowers appreciate moisture and a cool airy environment. Its scent increases mental agility and soothes loneliness. Rosemary is especially effective in love charms.

Rue (*Ruta graveolens*): Rue is a protective herb that successfully drives away all evil spirits and intents. Its unique dark green leaves and unforgettable odor confirm the herb's potent quality.

Santolina (*Santolina pinnata*): You'll not find this strange little plant mentioned in many herbals. Its coral-like form and silvery gray-green color marks santolina's individual nature. The Romans called it "ground cypress" and linked it to resurrection. Medieval lore declares santolina grants happiness and longevity.

THE WAY OF THE MOON

A New Moon rises with the Sun,
Her waxing half at midday shows,
The Full Moon climbs at sunset hour,
And waning half the midnight knows.

NEW	2005	FULL	NEW	2006	FULL
January 10		January 25	January 29		January 14
February 8		February 23	February 27		February 12
March 10		March 25	March 29		March 14
April 8		April 24	April 27		April 13
May 8		May 23	May 27		May 13
June 6		June 21	June 25		June 11
July 6		July 21	July 25		July 10
August 4		August 19	August 23		August 9
September 3		September 17	September 22		September 7
October 3		October 17	October 22		October 6
November 1		November 16	November 20		November 5
December 1/30		December 15	December 20		December 4

Life takes on added dimension when you match your activities to the waxing and waning of the Moon. Observe the sequence of her phases to learn the wisdom of constant change within complete certainty.

THE CELTIC TREE CALENDAR

Beth (Birch)	December 24 to January 20
Luis (Rowan)	January 21 to February 17
Nion (Ash)	February 18 to March 17
Fearn (Alder)	March 18 to April 14
Saille (Willow)	April 15 to May 12
Uath (Hawthorn)	May 13 to June 9
Duir (Oak)	June 10 to July 7
Tinne (Holly)	July 8 to August 4
Coll (Hazel)	August 5 to September 1
Muin (Vine)	September 2 to September 29
Gort (Ivy)	September 30 to October 27
Ngetal (Reed)	October 28 to November 24
Ruis (Elder)	November 25 to December 22

December 23 is not ruled by any tree for it is the "day" of the proverbial "year and day" in the earliest courts of law.

EARTH SIGNS

Taurus, Virgo, and Capricorn form the Earthy Trine of the zodiac circle. Ancient astrological lore assigned qualities to define the Earth element as nocturnal, negative, feminine, passive, cold and dry. Medieval mysticism added a melancholic nature. Modern astrology counters with a full capacity to enjoy earthly pleasures. All three signs are regarded as practical, strong, dependable and stubborn.

 TAURUS reigns during the height of the spring season and for this reason is designated as fixed, indicating stability. Key words such as patient, placid and reliable have long been used to describe the Bull. Sensuality, creativity and an appreciation of beauty are gifts of the love goddess, for Taurus owns the Night House of Venus.

VIRGO represents Persephone, virgin daughter of Demeter, goddess of agriculture, in classical mythology. The maiden's abduction marks the end of growing season and celebrates harvest. Although a mutable sign, one that spans two seasons, the gentle Virgin is defined as adaptable rather than unstable, for she belongs to the steadfast trine of Earth. Virgo occupies the Night Mansion of Mercury and his quicksilver gifts lend mental agility and deftness to the sign.

 CAPRICORN lives in the Night House of Saturn and many negative aspects accorded the Goat derive from Saturn's baleful influence. Saturn is the Roman equivalent of the Greek Titan Cronus, who devoured his own children. As the most remote planet in ancient days, Saturn ruled the coldest time of year, likened to the exiled Cronus when Zeus came to power. The Goat is a cardinal sign because it heralds winter and is endowed with authority, determination and inventiveness.

ELIZABETH PEPPER JOHN WILCOCK

To our readers,

One of the joys of publishing is reading our mail, so we always welcome your comments and observations. In the 1991 edition we sought your opinion to help us determine a production schedule for a series of future books. We suggested seven titles and asked that you let us know which interested you the most in order of preference. *Witches All*, an introduction to the craft, was the winner. An ambitious project, a decade passed before we were able to produce it. Not that we've been idle, you'll find many of the proposed books listed below.

The dawn of 2004 finds us entertaining the idea of a companion volume to *Witches All*—a book to further explore the depth and breadth of our fascinating subject. And we would appreciate knowing your particular interests and thoughts to guide us in the quest.

Every edition of the annual *Witches' Almanac* has included a coupon requesting your name and address. Please add your name to our files and keep in touch. We love to hear from you.

Address correspondence to P.O. Box 1292, Newport, RI 02840-9998.

The Editors

Our books available by mail order:

WITCHES ALL
This large glossy paperback is about the theory and practice of witchcraft, derived from past issues of *The Witches' Almanac*. It reveals the myriad ways an occultist uses to ensure health, wealth, and happiness—old ways as customs evolved.

A BOOK OF DAYS
John and Elizabeth celebrate the Seasons of Being with a collection of wise thoughts dealing with all aspects of human life, drawn from every source imaginable—from earliest records to the present, from Aristotle to Thurber. Quotations begin with Spring and Youth, then to Summer and Maturity, on to Autumn and Harvest, then Winter and Rest. Illustrated with over 200 medieval woodcuts.

MAGIC CHARMS FROM A TO Z
A treasury of amulets, talismans, fetishes and other lucky objects compiled by the staff of *The Witches' Almanac*. An invaluable guide for all who respond to the call of mystery and enchantment.

LOVE CHARMS
Love has many forms, many aspects. Ceremonies performed in witchcraft celebrate the joy and the blessings of love. Here is a collection of love charms to use now and ever after.

MAGICAL CREATURES
Mystic tradition grants pride of place to many members of the animal kingdom. Some share our life. Others live wild and free. Still others never lived at all, springing instead from the remarkable power of human imagination.

ANCIENT ROMAN HOLIDAYS
The glory that was Rome awaits you in Barbara Stacy's classic presentation of a festive year in pagan times. Here are the gods and goddesses as the Romans conceived them, accompanied by the annual rites performed in their worship. Scholarly, light-hearted—a rare combination.

CELTIC TREE MAGIC
Robert Graves in *The White Goddess* writes of the significance of trees in the old Celtic lore. *Celtic Tree Magic* is an investigation of the sacred trees in the remarkable Beth-Luis-Nion alphabet; their role in folklore, poetry, and mysticism.

MOON LORE
As both the largest and the brightest object in the night sky, and the only one to appear in phases, the Moon has been a rich source of myth for as long as there have been myth-makers.

MAGIC SPELLS AND INCANTATIONS
Words have magic power. Their sound, spoken or sung, has ever been a part of mystic ritual. From ancient Egypt to the present, those who practice the art of enchantment have drawn inspiration from a treasury of thoughts and themes passed down through the ages.

LOVE FEASTS
Creating meals to share with the one you love can be a sacred ceremony in itself. With the witch in mind, culinary adept Christine Fox offers magical menus and recipes for every month in the year.

RANDOM RECOLLECTIONS I, II, III, IV
Pages culled from the original (no longer available) issues of *The Witches' Almanac,* published annually throughout the 1970's, are now available in a series of tasteful booklets. A treasure for those who missed us the first time around; keepsakes for those who remember.

Order form on overleaf

Order Form

Each edition of *The Witches' Almanac* is a unique journey through the classic stylings of Elizabeth Pepper and John Wilcock. Limited numbers of previous years' editions are available.

____2004 - 2005 The Witches' Almanac @ $8.95_____

____2003 - 2004 The Witches' Almanac @ $8.95_____

____2002 - 2003 The Witches' Almanac @ $7.95_____

____2001 - 2002 The Witches' Almanac @ $7.95_____

____2000 - 2001 The Witches' Almanac @ $7.95_____

____1999 - 2000 The Witches' Almanac @ $7.95_____

____1998 - 1999 The Witches' Almanac @ $6.95_____

____1997 - 1998 The Witches' Almanac @ $6.95_____

____1996 - 1997 The Witches' Almanac @ $6.95_____

____1995 - 1996 The Witches' Almanac @ $6.95_____

____1994 - 1995 The Witches' Almanac @ $5.95_____

____1993 - 1994 The Witches' Almanac @ $5.95_____

____Celtic Tree Magic @ $6.95_____

____Love Charms @ $6.95_____

____Random Recollection I @ $3.95_____

____Random Recollection II @ $3.95_____

____Random Recollection III @ $3.95_____

____Random Recollection IV @ $3.95_____

____A Book of Days @ $15.95_____

____Moon Lore @ $7.95_____

____Love Feasts @ $6.95_____

____Ancient Roman Holidays @ $6.95_____

____Magic Charms from A to Z @ $12.95_____

____Magical Creatures @ $12.95_____

____Magic Spells and Incantations @ $12.95_____

____Witches' All @ $13.95_____

*Subtotal*_____

*Shipping & handling*_____

*Sales tax (RI orders only)*_____

*Total*_____

Shipping and handling charges: One book: $3.00 each additional book add $1.00

Send your name and address along with a check or money order payable in U. S. funds to: The Witches' Almanac, Ltd. PO Box 1292, Newport, RI 02840-9998